The Mystery of the Cross in the Present Planetary Transition

TRIGUEIRINHO

The Mystery of the Cross in the Present Planetary Transition

Editorial Revision by:
Artur de Paula Carvalho

Copyright © 2021 Jose Trigueirinho Netto

The profits generated from sales of books by Trigueirinho and his associates will be used to support the non-profit activities of the Shasti Association to disseminate their work.

Original Title in Portuguese:
O MISTÉRIO DA CRUZ NA ATUAL TRANSIÇÃO PLANETÁRIA
Copyright © 1992 by José Trigueirinho Netto

Translation and revision by John David Cutrell and Yatri (Frances O'Gorman, Ph. D.)

Cataloging-in-Publication data

Trigueririnho Netto, José
The Mystery of the Cross in the Present Planetary Transition
Trigueirinho. – Mount Shasta, CA, Shasti Association 2rd edition, 2021
132 p.
ISBN: 978-1-948430-09-8
Library of Congress Control Number: 2021930529
1. Spirituality
2. New Age
3. Occult Science
4. Christianity
I. Title.

English language rights reserved

Shasti Association
P.O. Box 318
Mt. Shasta, CA 96067-0318
editorial@shasti.org
www.shasti.org

Shasti Association

Preface

This book comes as the fruit of the work of a group that, on the inner levels, acts under the aegis of the spiritual Hierarchies. It is sent by the inner world in response to the need for teachings that can indicate the path toward the light in an ever-renewed way. It brings the seeds of future times and makes them available to beings whose consciousness should become fertile ground for the transformations that announce the new Earth.

Those who work as instruments to receive and materialize these writings know they are merely intermediaries. They silently express gratitude for the opportunity to serve altruistically.

May the readers who are devoted to the truth and who have divested themselves of concepts and expectations, venture along the paths of inner revelation and find the keys needed to open the portals along the way.

Trigueirinho
2003

Dedicated

*to those in the horizontal world of forms
who open themselves to the light that descends
vertically over them.*

*From the center of their being, and the center of this Cross,
may they bring about the redemption of matter
— the promise of the coming times.*

Contents

Introduction 11

Part 1
The Cross in the Symbolism of the Gospels

Symbols
The Meanings behind the Symbols 19
Symbols of the Gospels 23

Commentaries on the Symbols of the Gospels
Reflections and Clarifications 27
The Future 53

Part 2
Initiations in the Present Planetary Transition

Occult Aspects of the Initiations
The Initiations of Christ and of Jesus 59

The Occult Meaning of the Renunciation
of Christ and of Jesus 64

Initiations Today

Preliminary Considerations 69
The Process of Initiation in the Present Transition 72
Initiations and the Etheric Centers of a Being 82

Part 3
Epilogue

The Cross and Eternity

The Cross and the Path of Initiation 93
The Cross and the Four Elements 94
Awakening on Higher Levels 97

The Three Basic Forms of the Cross

Keys for Change 99
The Mutable Cross 100
The Fixed Cross 101
The Cardinal Cross 103

The Cross in the Coming Stage of the Earth

Preparing for the Coming Times 107
A Cristic Message 112

Introduction

The process of 'crucifixion' that the planet is undergoing is evident. However, those who know how to read between the lines of current illusory and chaotic reports can perceive a flow that is the essence of new life. As people understand this reality more deeply, they begin to partake of this energy that moves the great planetary transformation which is imminent. As they work toward this transformation, they dedicate themselves to it totally.

The transition of the Earth has already started and will culminate with its spiritual rebirth. The planetary Hierarchy[1] and those linked to it seek to fulfill the goal set for these times. This goal includes overcoming a state of lethargy and obscureness and guiding the planet, together with the beings who inhabit it, to a new and higher level of consciousness. However, the pangs of the birthing of this renewed life are unavoidable.

An energy of great power and beauty, of a silent yet steady radiation, penetrates each particle of the planetary universe and permeates all that is open to receive the brilliance that emanates

---

[1] **Planetary Hierarchy.** Consciousnesses that, from deep levels, guide planetary life to accomplish its spiritual purpose.

from it. It renews everything it touches with its ineffable love. Like leaven in bread, this energy multiplies the virtues of beings so that through them this suffering Earth can be nourished with light.

Humans cannot be exempt from compensating for their mistakes. Nevertheless, when they surrender to the truth, even if only partially, the spirit[2] sends them impulses of love, peace and wisdom. If received with gratitude, these energies will teach them how to gather flowers from among the rocks and transform the face of the Earth with their beauty.

When we consciously choose to 'crucify' our natural state, so steeped in selfishness, vanity, pride, animosity and arrogance, and allow the pure life inherent to our inner self to be expressed freely, we begin to know supreme blessedness, the nonmaterial treasure that nothing in the world can profane.

The duality that still prevails in the outer life of the surface of the Earth causes many conflicts. This duality is used in the midst of chaos and disharmony as an instrument for humans to be tested and to learn, bringing them countless opportunities for elevation. In these times the call is renewed for humans to rediscover the limitless Source of life. Issuing forth since the beginning of time, this call has continued to reverberate throughout the ages and it increased with the incarnation of Christ[3] two thousand years ago. Now it is breaking down the obstacles inflicted by individualism and is seeking to resonate deeply within each person.

---

[2] **Spirit.** The nucleus of consciousness of the being on cosmic levels of manifestation; the monad.

[3] **Christ.** The Entity whose consciousness reaches the level of divine fulfillment that is possible for a human being. In Jesus, Christ expressed the Second Cosmic Ray in a unique way and to a degree never before attained on the surface of the Earth. The term Christ often refers to this energy itself and not necessarily to the Entity that manifested it.

Three great portals open up to those who respond to this call, marking the beginning of the path that will lead humans to finally become part of the spiritual kingdom. In the course of evolution all human beings will go through these portals. The opportunity today is unique because once the first portal is crossed, the way to the others becomes shorter.

These three preliminary portals consist of:

- elevating one's activity so that it becomes increasingly directed by the inner self;
- purifying that part of one's being related to emotions, transmuting desire into aspiration and channeling that aspiration toward spiritual life;
- focusing the mind on the light of the soul,[4] which by then will have reached a clear and unwavering attunement with the light of the monad.[5]

Through the soul, the inner self begins to control its physical-material expression and to govern the actions of the personality. This control is exercised according to the receptivity of the personality. When observing their own lives, many recognize they are truly directed by a higher transcendent will, a will that acts in an invisible way and guides their steps to unimaginable destinies.

After having attained some control over the actions of the personality, the inner self gradually extends that control to feelings and thoughts until it is assured that the personality, now as a cohesive nucleus, is responding reliably to spiritual impulses on the three levels of human existence. At this point, individuals are

---

[4] **Soul.** Nucleus of the being's consciousness that is manifested on the causal level. The focus of the soul is currently transferring from the abstract mental level to the intuitive level (see diagram on page 70).

[5] **Monad.** The nucleus of the being's consciousness on cosmic levels of manifestation; also called the spirit.

assigned a task to collaborate with the Hierarchy. Through service, their consciousness ascends rapidly. At a certain stage one can say that individuals no longer belong to the kingdom of humans, for they have confirmed their affiliation with the source of spiritual life and have found their dwelling place in it. As servers of the light, their steps are determined by the call of the spirit; their way leads toward those who need them. The Emerald Tablet,[6] found by an Initiate on the body of Hermes, contained the following inscription:

> *Separate the earth from the fire, the subtle from the gross...*
> *Ascend...from the earth to heaven, and then again descend to earth...*

To give of oneself completely is a quality of the monad. But there are very few humans who express the energy of the monadic level and the virtues that stem from it, in a crystalline way. In these times the great majority have not yet even awakened to the life of the soul. Only a small but significant number are able to reflect the will of their higher nucleus, the monad. The opportunity now being offered is available to all. Each one, at his or her own level of evolution, receives an impulse to ascend. Whenever some obsolete aspect is renounced and one's surrender is perfected, one undergoes a crucifixion and the ensuing rebirth.

There are many levels of crucifixion. However, this term is used esoterically to express a specific state in which the essence of the human mental, emotional and physical-etheric bodies has merged into the body of the soul, the causal body. The soul seeks to draw nearer to spiritual and divine energy and 'crucifies itself',

---

[6] **The Emerald Tablet.** Original source of Hermetic Philosophy and Alchemy, a document well-known to scholars and occult philosophers since the 10th century. See *Tabula Smaragdina, Emerald Tablet of Hermes Trigmagistus*, translated from Latin by John Stahl [Legget, CA: The Evanescent Press, 1988, http://cscs.umich.edu/~crshalizi/smaragdina.html], pages 7 and 8.

which is to say, it renounces everything that pertains to its own level of existence. Therefore, by 'dying' to that which is known, it is reborn to a new life, to spiritual life. For this reason the Initiation[7] symbolized by the crucifixion is also known as the *great renunciation*.

Such is the mystery of the cross. Those who lay themselves down upon the cross, those who from its center let illusion fade away, by the perfect equilibrium between the shaft that is raised and the beam that remains horizontal, reconcile the opposites within themselves. Nurtured by surrender and sustained by wisdom, they embrace the flower of compassion, the flower that prefigures the fruits of eternity.

---

[7] **Initiation.** In esoteric language this term is used to designate a specific process of expansion of consciousness that marks a being's passage into more subtle levels of energy.

Part 1

The Cross in the Symbolism of the Gospels

Symbols

The Meaning behind the Symbols

The pathway followed by humanity[1] of the surface of the Earth has led it to become so strongly identified with the outer side of life that its contact with subtle worlds and with the hidden symbols in material existence has practically disappeared.

In general, the experiences lived in dreams and the impressions brought by the subtle senses are considered symbolic and they represent realities from the inner worlds. However, what happens in life in the awakened state, when the one's faculties are active on the physical level, is not always considered to be symbolic. If humans of the surface were truly aware of the ephemeral nature of the world of forms, the way they approach daily life would be very different because external events also represent broader inner realities. Symbols contain a synthesis of timeless realities, therefore they transcend the chronology of the material

---

[1] **Humanity.** A form of life that is present on various levels of consciousness throughout the universes. Humanity is not limited to physical worlds or to the surface of planets. This book is concerned with humanity of the surface of planet Earth.

world. Under veils, they safeguard insights that may be understood by using different keys.

According to H.P.B.,[2] every symbol is kept under seven keys and each key must be turned seven times. Therefore, a symbol is directly related to the levels of consciousness and may be understood in the light of seven times seven energies. H.P.B. also said that in the 19th Century, when she wrote *The Secret Doctrine*,[3] only three of these keys were available to humanity.

Throughout this book indications are given that can lead students to discover these keys, which are related to the following fields of knowledge: anthropology, astrology, astronomy, physics or physiology, geometry, metaphysics, mysticism, numerology and psychology.

In the present planetary transition, many sections of the akashic records,[4] which in the past were hidden except to advanced Initiates from the Fifth Initiation upward, are now becoming accessible as of the Third Initiation. In rare cases, some contacts with these records may be established even by second level Initiates under the sponsorship of a Hierarchy.

This increased access to the akashic records reverberates throughout the planetary environs. Thus, humans are able to more clearly perceive matters that were previously incomprehensible to

---

[2] **H.P.B.** Helena Petrovna Blavatsky (1831 — 1891). A mystic whose tasks included providing human beings with a basis for occult wisdom, thus permitting them to develop a synthesis of various spiritual tendencies of the planet. Ever since the mid-nineteenth century this groundwork has been preparing for the emergence of mental unity among the humans of the surface of the Earth. The work of H.P.B. launched a stage that brought the Hierarchy closer to the life of this humanity.

[3] See Helena P. Blavatsky, *The Secret Doctrine: The Synthesis of Science, Religion and Philosophy*, vol. I — *Cosmogenesis* and vol. II — *Anthropogenesis* [London: The Theosophical Publishing Company, Limited, 1888].

[4] **Akashic records.** States of consciousness where information about the entire Universe, from the beginning of its manifestation to its return to uncreated worlds, is imprinted.

them and to enter into heretofore unattainable regions of consciousness. This is especially true of rescuable beings,[5] for in some way they have responded to the impulse of inner light. In other words, this process brings Heaven down closer to Earth and takes Earth up closer to Heaven.

The outer life of an Initiate is a much more crystalline reflection of the inner reality that motivates, guides and sustains him or her than the life of the average person. Moreover, the more one's energy penetrates higher consciousness, the wider is the range of vibrations that one manifests. Each action will bring with it the basic energy of the levels where one's consciousness is awakened. Thus, life can be understood in infinite ways, depending on the angle from which it is approached. The same event can be perceived in various ways that complement, rather than contradict, one another.

The meaning of a symbol that is perceived intuitively will not tend to be distorted if the individual acting as the channel has transcended the limitations imposed by dense matter. This is true, even if for only those special moments of intuitive reception when one's consciousness is absorbed by the aura of a Hierarchy.

The conceptualization of a symbol has its roots in nonmaterial levels of existence and the definition of its form embodies many currents of energy. The higher the focus of the consciousness of the one who intuitively perceives the symbol, the purer will be the image projected on the individual's inner mirror. If the perceived form does not reflect the essence of nonmaterial energy, that symbol will generally tend to become devitalized because it will be divested of reality.

---

[5] **Rescuable beings.** Beings of the various kingdoms existing on Earth that are capable of responding to evolutionary stimuli and of becoming part of that portion of planetary life that will remain unscathed during the more intense cataclysms of the present transition.

Each cycle expresses its own energies and is composed of patterns corresponding to specific archetypes that should serve to update the manifestation of life. Thus, because of their great capacity to contain abstract and synthesized energies, symbols are especially important instruments to stimulate the patterns to be implanted in each new evolutionary stage.

When a symbol is made known to humans by the Hierarchy, it comes to accomplish an energy work on the material levels of the planet. In such cases it brings the vibration of higher patterns of behavior that humanity is to incorporate.

Certain events in the life of Jesus represent stages of Initiation. What happened to Christ, while in Jesus, from the arrest to the resurrection,[6] also corresponds to specific phases in the present planetary transition. To understand this, one must read the same symbolic events from different perspectives.

This transition is such an extensive process and has such deep repercussions on the evolution of the entire planet, as well as on the solar system, that its true significance has generally not yet been understood by rescuable beings. When the reality of this transition is perceived, its essence is usually distorted by the egotism still present in the beings. This makes them focus only on their own salvation and on the salvation of persons close to them. Nevertheless, the opportunity that has been, is, and will go on being offered to humans of the surface of the Earth, is much greater.

Happy are those who have not seen and yet believe.
(John 20:29)

✧ ✧ ✧

---

[6] **Resurrection.** One of the most occult inner processes for humans of the surface of the Earth. In the present planetary transition and also in the cycle that ended on 8/8/88 (August 8, 1988), the complete experience of this process takes place when a being reaches the Seventh Initiation and is integrated into the Solar Hierarchy.

Symbols of the Gospels

Over time, the original texts of the Gospels have been altered for different reasons, such as the limitations of some translators who were not Initiates and could not discern the correct significance. This could also have been due to the limitations of modern languages, which do not have an adequate vocabulary to express certain inner realities, or even due to the intention of certain individuals to perpetuate their dogmas and control the ignorant masses. Even so, in the current versions of these texts we can still find certain symbolic passages that make it possible to get a little closer to the truth hidden in the manifestation of Christ. It is important to emphasize that the energy permeating these passages is not present in the written words, but it emerges from contact with the source that gave rise to the facts described there. Therefore, the goal of a revelatory study is not to know the facts in themselves, but rather to build a bridge to the life that sustains the entire Tree of Creation.

The process lived by Christ, in Jesus, from his arrest to his resurrection, a process that is mirrored in the present times, can be summed up in seven stages.[7]

First stage – the arrest: betrayal by humanity

✧ Jesus goes with his disciples to a garden.

---

[7] **Seven Stages.** The episodes cited here are from the *Gospels of Matthew* (26:36 to 28:15), *Mark* (14:32 to 16:11), *Luke* (22:39 to 24:12) and *John* (18:1 to 20:18). All quotations are taken from *The Jerusalem Bible, Reader's Edition* [Garden City, NY: Doubleday and Company, Inc., 1966].

- Judas, who was a disciple of Jesus but who betrays him, approaches Jesus together with officials of the court and soldiers provided by the pontiffs and the Pharisees.
- Jesus identifies himself to the soldiers twice and urges his disciples not to react.
- The disciples abandon Jesus and run away.
- Jesus is taken before the high priest.

Second stage – the judgment: human choices

- Jesus is taken to the tribunals and placed before Pilate and the priests; he is unjustly accused but makes no reply.
- Pilate is warned by his wife that Jesus is innocent, for this had been shown to her in a dream, but Pilate pays no heed.
- Peter, a disciple of Jesus, denies three times that he knows him.
- The mob is asked if it wants Jesus or the notorious criminal, Barabbas, to be set free; the mob chooses to free Barabbas.
- Pilate 'washes his hands'.
- The soldiers tear off Jesus' garments and cover him with a red cape; they make a crown of thorns and put it on his head; they scoff at him, spit in his face, and beat him with sticks.
- The mob takes on the crucifixion of Jesus.

Third stage – the way of the cross: a being's gradual awakening

- ✧ Simon of Cyrene carries the cross of Jesus to Golgotha.
- ✧ Along the way, Jesus tells the women who were grieving not to weep for him but rather for themselves and their descendents, for the day will surely come when it will be said: "Happy are those who are barren, the wombs that have never borne...for if men use the green wood like this, what will happen when it is dry?" (Luke 23: 28-31)

Fourth stage – the crucifixion: sacrifice as a means of transmutation

- ✧ The soldiers offer Jesus wine mixed with gall to drug him but he refuses to drink it.
- ✧ The soldiers take Jesus' garments and divide them among themselves by casting lots; they stand watch around the cross on which Jesus has been nailed.
- ✧ Two criminals are crucified on either side of Jesus; one blasphemes against him and the other defends him.
- ✧ Those passing by revile Jesus, insulting and scorning him.
- ✧ The sky darkens for three hours, then Jesus says: "It is accomplished..." (John 19:30), and dies.

Fifth stage – the final moments on Golgotha: the inevitable reaction

- The veil of the temple is torn in two from top to bottom; the earth trembles, rocks are split, tombs open and many righteous come back to life.

Sixth stage – the burial: a new opportunity for those who remained silent

- Joseph of Arimathaea, an eminent member of the council that condemned Jesus, but who did not agree with the decision, takes it upon himself to bury the body of Jesus in a new tomb.
- The priests send guards to keep watch over the tomb.

Seventh stage – the resurrection: the new times are prefigured

- Three days go by after the burial; Mary Magdalene and some other women go to the tomb where Jesus has been laid and find it open; an angel tells them that Jesus has come back to life.
- Jesus appears to Mary Magdalene revealing to her that he was ascending to the Father.

Commentaries on the Symbols of the Gospels

Reflections and Clarifications

A rare gift was bestowed on human beings when their mental abilities were awakened. Through these abilities, humans could contact inner and spiritual realities and relate to material life according to higher laws. In this way, they could aid the development of humankind in general. However, this gift contained a test: its value would only be revealed if humans used it to benefit universal harmony.

The supreme consciousness that governs this planet has always sent its Messengers in order to transmit to humanity the eternal truths and precepts that would guide it on the paths of integrity and peace.

The coming of Christ to the material levels began the culmination of an important phase of this process.

This phase reaches its completion in the present planetary

transition, in what is esoterically referred to as *the reappearance of the Christ*.[1]

The Logos,[2] which is the governing consciousness of a planet, can follow different paths in its evolution. The Logos that governed Earth in the stage now coming to a close, took the Path of Sacrifice.[3] This option was extended to all the Hierarchy, who transmit and carry out the Logoic purpose. Thus, the cross is the symbol of the perfect interrelationship between material existence (the horizontal beam) and inner, spiritual and cosmic life (the upright shaft of the cross). The cross hides its mystery in the deepest essence of planetary life, the essence that undertook the task of establishing harmony and equilibrium among apparently opposing expressions of energy.

By taking part in the task of bringing together spirit and matter on Earth, Christ, as a channel of manifestation of love-wisdom, gave witness to the ineffable self-abnegation of the planetary Logos. This process is extremely dynamic. In bringing down that which is above, it raises up that which is below, without ever acceding to the vibration of the material levels. In this way, Christ affirmed before Pilate:

Mine is not a kingdom of this world…(John 18:36)

---

[1] **The reappearance of the Christ.** The return of the cristic energy among humans as prophesied in spiritual teachings. This reappearance refers to the awakening of the cristic flame, the inner Christ, that is taking place in many beings of the rescuable portion of humanity.

[2] **Logos.** A planetary Logos is the nucleus that governs the existence of a planet. It is from this Logos that all planetary life and the diverse consciousnesses of which it is composed, receive the sustenance that nurtures them and gives them the impulse to follow the path of evolution.

[3] **Path of Sacrifice**. The way chosen by the beings who give themselves completely to the work of supporting the manifestation of the sacred purpose of life on all levels. The negative connotation of sacrifice is being replaced by a sense of the true inner reality of the term that implies the fulfillment of a sacred inner task.

First stage – the arrest: betrayal by humanity

Jesus goes with his disciples to a garden.

Two thousand years ago the cristic energy[4] was present in humanity through Jesus. It was expressed in the most complete way possible for that time by a being incarnated on the physical level of the surface of Earth. Nevertheless, the majority of humankind refused to accept it.

Something similar is currently taking place. Only ten percent of all humanity of the surface respond positively to the cristic call that has been echoing for millennia and that is present again in a special way during this transition of the Earth.

The ones who respond are the disciples of light; they recognize the light of love and wisdom. Their becoming one with this light does not depend on beliefs, dogmas or organized religions; it is built on unification with the cosmic cristic essence. Those who respond, unite on supraphysical levels, gathered around this sublime energy which governs all the twelve inner groups.[5]

---

[4] **Cristic energy.** The energy of love-wisdom, a synthesis of the vibrations emitted by the spiritual center of this solar system. This energy has an immanent nature of attraction that contributes to drawing all this systemic universe toward its inner life, the source that sustains it. Christ is the consciousness that represents this intangible and sublime energy to a high degree of perfection.

[5] **Inner groups.** Nuclei of consciousness intimately linked to higher evolution on the planetary level. Twelve inner groups are active on Earth; each one expresses a Ray energy and takes on the portion of the planetary purpose which that Ray is to fulfill through the human kingdom.

Judas, who was a disciple of Jesus but who betrays him, approaches Jesus together with officials of the court and soldiers provided by the pontiffs and the Pharisees.

The paths leading to the spirit have always been open to all human beings. Nevertheless, the majority have preferred the allurement of material life and have betrayed what should be the purpose of their existence for the sake of false promises.

The Hierarchy stimulates the awakening of one's consciousness using the best means available to help each being. Furthermore, the spirit uses the most penetrating means possible to reach human consciousness. However, aspirations toward inner life often do not find openness to their expression in material existence. As has been said: "The Spirit is willing, but the flesh is weak." (Matthew 26:41)

Human beings have lost awareness of their own actions because they have opted for the pleasures of the senses and for earthly power; they have become obsessed by forces of dissuasion and dazzled by illusions. Deluded, they have handed the life of the planet over to destruction. As Christ said: "The Son of Man is going to his fate, as the scriptures say he will, but alas for that man by whom the Son of Man will be betrayed! Better for that man if he had never been born!" (Matthew 26:24)

✧ ✧ ✧

Jesus identifies himself to the soldiers twice and urges his disciples not to react.

Cristic energy is not hidden from anyone's view. It is present in the smallest events of people's lives, pointing the way to Unity and seeking to dissolve separateness and strife. This is very little understood, even among would-be followers.

The supreme wisdom of cristic energy seeks to awaken in humanity the awareness that true existence, the Kingdom, is to be found beyond the thresholds of the mind. The life of the Spirit is the portal to this existence and individuals are guided to it along paths charted by infinite love. But only those who continually renounce the violence of their own ego[6] are able to go through this portal.

✧ ✧ ✧

The disciples abandon Jesus and run away.

Countless times during the process of terrestrial evolution humans are brought face to face with the Truth, the Light and the Life. In some of these opportunities they are able to break through the dense veils of illusion that darken their consciousness. This evokes a positive response from their most intimate inner core, an opening and a step toward spiritual life. However, this still fragile commitment to the inner call is often forsaken when trials arise.

Humans often forget that the manifestation of a new existence requires deeds and actions in keeping with the inspiration for such a way of life. The foundations for this new existence can only emerge from a heart where love has transcended personal expression, a heart which recognizes that all of this love comes

---

[6] **Ego.** Nucleus of consciousness on the human level that holds within itself the sense of "I." It is a projection of the soul on this level. The ego manipulates the forces of the personality (synthesis of the individual's past on material levels) that by nature manifests egoism and a tendency to be identified with the illusory world of forms. The destiny of the ego is to be absorbed into the soul in the course of evolution and from then on the inner energy of the being is expressed with greater freedom.

from the One Who gives life to the universes and to Whom all must be offered. Those who become one with this love fear nothing. Whether in the heavens or on Earth, they share in the unity of the Source and ephemeral things cannot wrest eternity away from them.

Nonetheless, the history of the Earth reveals that human beings have not understood these simple spiritual laws. The influence that concrete objects and concepts have on them is stronger than their faith in the providence and mercy of the inner levels. They fear losing what is ephemeral and consequently they cast aside what is essential. They propagate their beliefs but their actions seldom bear witness to those beliefs.

This humanity alleges to have reached a level of evolution that leads it to believe it has attained a very high state of consciousness and has performed great deeds. But how many are able to remain faithful to the inner goal of their life when assailed by material forces?

✧ ✧ ✧

Jesus is taken before the high priest.

There is an archetype for the structures that underlie the development of a civilization. When these structures are built on this archetype, they reflect cosmic order. However, they must be continually readjusted to the higher thought from which they emanate, otherwise these structures become crystallized and are used as instruments of the forces of involution.

For the most part, the structures maintained by humans in the life of the surface of the Earth have tended to digress from the thought that inspired them. Furthermore, from the very beginning, the vast majority of humans have succumbed to negative purposes. Therefore, the everyday lives of individuals, as well as religious organizations and official institutions, have become targeted by the actions of forces of dissuasion. What was meant to be the repository and radiating core of light on concrete levels, became enshrouded by the smoke of material fires.

✧ ✧ ✧

Second stage – the judgment: human choices

*Jesus is taken to the tribunals
and placed before Pilate and the priests;
he is unjustly accused, but makes no reply.*

Throughout the ages the Logos of the Earth has been granting human beings the best possible conditions for their development. It has offered the resources of the planet, opening its wellsprings to them, giving them everything they needed. However, in return for so many gifts, humans embarked on the path of plunder and selfish squandering. They handed the planet over to the forces that are trying to destroy it. Nevertheless, planetary life keeps on giving of itself unceasingly.

The Logos of the Earth is closely linked to cristic energy. Thus, what happens on the planetary body[7] is, in an occult sense, imprinted on the cristic line of light that governs the existence of

---

[7] **Planetary body.** A group of particles, on various levels of existence, through which the essence of a planetary Logos is manifested.

the Earth and the solar system. As Christ said: "I am the Light of the World." (John 8:12)

✧ ✧ ✧

> *Pilate is warned by his wife that Jesus is innocent,*
> *for this had been shown to her in a dream;*
> *but Pilate pays no heed.*

The powerful impulse of giving, which comes from the essence of life, stimulates the awakening of all beings. It excludes no one and is poured over the entire Earth, reaching its farthest corners. The governing consciousness of the planet, together with its Hierarchy, has taken on the laborious task of redeeming earthly life. This is implicit in the words of Jesus: "You did not choose me, no, I chose you." (John 15:16)

This impulse of giving is perceived by a few humans. Some of those who find themselves entangled in the play of material forces, recognize the truth hidden behind external events. However, they often do not have enough energy to break the negative ties that bind them or they are unable to follow a pure path because of the resistance of matter itself. They know the truth but cannot do anything about it.

✧ ✧ ✧

> *Peter, a disciple of Jesus,*
> *denies three times that he knows him.*

Humans whose knowledge is limited to material consciousness[8] and who are caught up in extreme illusion and involvement with the forces of involution, have difficulty contacting their inner origins. Thus, they reject the possibility of being touched by these origins and hence forsake their divine filiation.

Even those who have been able to recognize the immanence of the cristic energy and have cherished its presence within themselves, tend to reject, on the mental, emotional and physical-etheric levels of their personality, the innermost principles of their own consciousness. In these times of transition, when the forces of dissuasion strongly assail rescuable beings, one must be vigilant and walk faithfully toward the Light.

✧ ✧ ✧

> *The mob is asked if it wants Jesus or the*
> *notorious criminal, Barabbas, to be set free;*
> *the mob chooses to free Barabbas.*

Human beings have continually been given the possibility of choosing higher ways of living. They have persistently been called to unite with The One who gave them existence. However, mesmerized by the constant din of voices that promise pleasure and delight, they have not heard the Call.

---

[8] **Material consciousness.** Consciousness on the material levels: mental, emotional and physical-etheric.

In these times of transition, above all, the great majority allow themselves to be seduced by an already corrupt material world and obstinately resist the inflow of the energy of the spirit. This increasingly opens the way for domination by the forces of involution.

✧ ✧ ✧

Pilate 'washes his hands'.

Those who have remained recalcitrant to the Call until the end of this planetary phase will understand the words of Christ: "You will look for me and will not find me: where I am you cannot come." (John 7:34)

In the twentieth century the planetary Hierarchy attempted in a special way to draw near to the principal leaders of the nations of the world, sending them its messengers. Furthermore, when it was still possible for this civilization to reverse its escalating degradation and when karmic conditions permitted, the Hierarchy also attempted to stimulate some people having links with it to hold key positions in the governments of the nations. But the talons of vanity and of ambition, the misuse of power and the illusion of material goods had strongly infiltrated the hearts of humankind. So, in spite of all these efforts, the governments that should have reflected the inner regency of the planet,[9] yielded to the pressures of the forces of chaos.

✧ ✧ ✧

---

[9] **Inner regency of the planet.** The inner central regent consciousness of a planet is its Logos. This regency has nuclei that are in charge of carrying planetary evolution forward. The Lord of the World (the consciousness that expresses the will aspect of the logoic energy) and the planetary Hierarchy are among the more important of these nuclei.

The soldiers tear off Jesus' garments and cover him with a red cape;
they make a crown of thorns and place it on his head;
they scoff at him, spit in his face, and beat him with sticks.

In the past, there were periods on Earth in which the rulers were directly linked to, or were even members of, the planetary Hierarchy. As external life entered into a phase of greater density and humans gradually gave in to the forces of involution, the likelihood of humanity relating to the Hierarchy was curtailed. The incongruity between the goals of the leaders of the nations and the goals of the inner regency of the planet caused many human beings to became easy prey to the forces of evil.

The destruction brought on by these forces of involution has become more prevalent in the human lives. Flames of criminal fires have reddened the skies of the planet. Reckless extraction of natural resources has scarred the planet's outer layers. The continual disgorging of waste and sewage onto the land and into the waters has contaminated the sources of water. Wars and testing of weapons have caused the destruction of both the material and the subtle life of many areas of the planet.

✧ ✧ ✧

The mob takes on the crucifixion of Jesus.

If higher will had not intervened in this process, the planet would have been destroyed, causing an immense imbalance in the entire solar system and in the galaxy. When the action of this higher will comes into full force, humankind will be able to have a better understanding of these words of Jesus: "...the hour has come: glorify your Son..." (John 17:1) However, until this time arrives, most humans do not seem willing to refrain from taking part in the destruction. Thus, humanity takes the path that would lead to the extinction of life on the surface of the Earth if it were not for this higher intervention.

❖ ❖ ❖

Third stage – the way of the cross: the being's gradual awakening

Simon of Cyrene carries the cross of Jesus to Golgotha.

As the planetary situation goes on deteriorating, many consciousnesses belonging to the Brotherhood of Light[10] have come to the aid of the Earth. The essence of this Brotherhood sends forth love-wisdom, granting those who are part of it the ability to radiate this omniscient healing energy to points of the cosmos that must be reached. The central regency of the cosmos assigns the tasks to be performed by the Brotherhood. The aim of these tasks during acute situations, such as those being lived on the Earth today, is expressed in the words spoken by Christ to the Father: "...may they [humankind] be so completely one that the world will realize that it was you who sent me and that I have loved them as much as you loved me." (John 17:23)

---

[10] **Brotherhood of Light.** A network of energies and consciousnesses that has its base on cosmic levels and extends throughout the entire universe. It works to bring about the manifestation of the Plan of Evolution. The beings that form this network respond in a positive way to the impulse sent by the Center of Creation.

The Logos of Earth and its Hierarchy constitute one of the innumerable prolongations of this Brotherhood. Whenever needed, and according to highest designs, elevated consciousnesses affiliated with this Brotherhood are called upon to operate in different points of the cosmos. This kind of collaboration has never ceased to exist on this planet. Many ancient writings refer to this fact in a veiled way. There were occasions in which the continuity of life on concrete levels of the Earth was endangered. The cosmic Brotherhood is present in a special way during critical times, endeavoring to heal the imbalances that the planet is suffering.

✧ ✧ ✧

Along the way, Jesus tells the women who were grieving not to weep for him but rather for themselves and their descendents, for the day will surely come when it will be said: "Happy are those who are barren, the wombs that have never born... for if men use the green wood like this, what will happen when it is dry?" (Luke 23: 28-31)

Aspirants who awaken to inner realities and become aware of the present planetary situation can easily get caught up in illusions. Thus, they might try to solve problems that can only be solved by a higher energy. Until peace abides within them, people can do very little to further peace in the world around them. Until they overcome selfishness, they cannot contribute to the manifestation of love and unity among their fellow beings. What they create cannot really reflect divine purpose until they have been able to penetrate the secrets of Creation.

When procreation results from gratification or from a veiled expectation of self-achievement through one's children, the karmic debts[11] of the parents are increased and they also take on the karma that comes from the beings who incarnated through them.

Thus, karmic ties between parents and children are directly reflected in their process of evolution. In certain cases, procreation that takes place outside of spiritual laws can slow down the evolution of the incarnating person as well as that of the parents, for the entire incarnation. Spiritual energy encounters obstacles in vitalizing the bodies that will receive the incarnating being and also partially withdraws from the parents. The life-flow that should nurture the being's higher development is thus blocked or withdrawn. So, the person's life will be little more than dry wood. The play of forces of involution can easily deceive those who lack the inner renewal brought by this spiritual life-flow.

✧ ✧ ✧

Fourth stage – the crucifixion: sacrifice as a means of transmutation

The soldiers offer Jesus wine mixed with gall to drug him but he refuses to drink it.

---

[11] **Karmic debt.** The law of karma, also called the law of cause and effect, governs the evolution of human beings whose consciousness is focused on material levels. It states that every action calls for an equal reaction in order to maintain the equilibrium of the universe. Individuals who do not awaken to inner life remain prisoners of the material world due to their many negative actions. This is karmic debt. See Trigueirinho, *Beyond Karma* [Minas Gerais, Brazil: Irdin Editora, 2003].

Many times the fraternity of darkness has tried to induce the beings connected to the Hierarchy to give in to its maleficent purposes. Those whose inner ties remain firm in the face of the assault of these negative forces are tempted by them to venture into situations that would separate them from the truth, but they rarely give in.

A fact still unknown to most of humanity is that at a certain point during the Middle Ages, when the forces of involution pervaded the material levels to such an extent that they could control a large part of the thoughts, feelings and acts of human beings, the fraternity of darkness proposed a pact with the spiritual Hierarchy of the planet. By means of this pact, the destruction being caused by agents of darkness would be alleviated if they would be allowed to penetrate more freely into the level of the soul. This proposal was not even taken into consideration. The stance of the Hierarchy was — and will be, in the final hours — the living example of compliance with Higher Law, the total fulfillment of the words: "…(Father), your Will be done!" (Matthew 26:42)

What occurred hundreds of years ago was directly reflected in the great confrontation on the surface of the planet in the twentieth century (referred to as the World Wars), a confrontation in which the destiny of the Earth was at stake.

✧ ✧ ✧

The soldiers take Jesus' garments
and divide them among themselves by casting lots;
they stand watch around the cross on which Jesus has been nailed.

In esoteric symbolism the soul represents the Son and its destiny is to become united with the monad, the Father. This gives us a hint of what is meant by the following words of Jesus: "...the Son can do nothing of himself; he can do only what he sees the Father doing..." (John 5:19), or: "...if you did know me, you would know my Father as well..." (John 8:19) and also: "my glory is conferred by the Father..." (John 8:54)

The soul holds the mental, emotional and physical-etheric permanent atoms[12] in its aura. Because of its interaction with the dense levels of existence (mental, emotional and physical-etheric), the soul's task of linking matter and spirit is limited until matter recognizes and surrenders to the omnipotence of the spirit.

When the monad activates the potential of the soul by applying its will intensely enough to elevate the soul in power and energy, the soul becomes able to 'crucify the ego' and to free itself from the play of forces of destruction and chaos which engulf most human beings. This liberation corresponds to the rescue[13] that is occurring today to the retrievable portion of this humanity. Rescue takes place in the core of the being who is focused on a level that is free of the action of the forces of involution, a process that may or may not include the dense bodies. On the external, material levels, the forces of involution will go on acting more aggressively until the end of the present planetary transition. The civilization of the surface of the Earth is going through a corresponding process on a planetary scale. Its 'soul' is being rescued to a higher level and will 'incarnate' in new vestments at a future stage.

---

[12] **Permanent atoms.** Nuclei that synthesize the energy and the experience of the dense mental, emotional and physical-etheric bodies. There is one permanent atom for each of these bodies. Through these nuclei the soul is able to introduce subtle impulses into external life.

[13] **Rescue.** A process that is taking the Earth to more elevated levels of energy and that has the participation of extra-planetary consciousnesses. Those beings who are to inhabit the Earth after this harmonization will have an affinity with the new energy that will then be manifested.

The external forms of religious and philosophical teachings revealed by cristic beings[14] through the ages have given form to the essential truth of existence during past stages of this civilization. Dark forces take over these forms and use them as instruments of their work of dissuasion, a characteristic of the present times of transition.

✧ ✧ ✧

Two criminals are crucified on either side of Jesus; one blasphemes against him and the other defends him.

Two thousand years ago there were three crosses on Calvary. On one cross hung a being who embodied spiritual and divine energies; on another, a criminal who recognized the light, the truth and life in this being; on the third, another criminal who repudiated this being. Likewise, humans today have three nuclei of consciousness that express clearly defined states: the monad, the soul and the ego (see diagram on page 70). The monad is pure in essence and reflects the cosmic origin of the human being. The soul is able to recognize the immanent truth of the monad but, since it is manifested on the abstract mental level, it is not totally free from the deceit and from the onslaught of evil or from involvement with it. The ego expresses the distortions still inherent in earthly matter. Until the fire of spirit permeates the ego and sets it aflame, the illusion of separateness makes the ego prey to these temptations and to that which is referred to as evil.

✧ ✧ ✧

---

[14] **Cristic beings.** Beings who express cristic energy to a degree of purity that is capable of producing inner changes in the consciousness of human beings and of the planet.

*Those passing by revile Jesus,
insulting and scorning him.*

To surrender one's ego to crucifixion implies treading the path of renunciation, of self-oblivion and of equanimity in the face of both pleasure and of pain. It is the path of abdicating one's own concepts. All these things are normally little understood by the world. The forces of evil dominate the great majority of earthly humans; therefore, they cannot be expected to embrace the light with gratitude.

The scorn hurled by the world at those who seek the light is one of the tests that disciples[15] must undergo. Nothing must change their willingness to surrender to inner life. To them Jesus addressed these words: "If the world hates you, remember that it hated me before you. If you belonged to the world, the world would love you as its own; but because you do not belong to the world, because my choice withdrew you from the world, therefore the world hates you." (John 15:18) "The world hates me because I give evidence that its ways are evil." (John 7:7)

*The sky darkens for three hours, then Jesus says:
"It is accomplished..." (John 19:30) and dies.*

Numbers are symbols of many processes. For example, the

---

[15] **Disciple.** An individual who, in response to the inner self, elevates his or her patterns of behavior and draws near to the aura of a Hierarchy, thus preparing to attain the First Initiation. In general, this term is used to designate beings, whether or not they are Initiates, who are instructed spiritually by consciousnesses of a vibration higher than their own.

number three corresponds to the primeval triad[16] and veils the mystery of the "three that are one." This archetype of multiplicity and unity (3 and 1) corresponds to the soul's assimilation of the synthesis of the three bodies of the personality.

In referring to this period of darkness of three hours or, as the prophecies of the end times predict, that of three days, it is important to point out that periods such as these generally do not correspond to concrete physical reality, but rather to a darkening of the three levels of manifestation. If the peak of such a period, which for human consciousness is likened to darkness, happens to coincide with phenomena that produce the absence of sunlight on the material level, (something perfectly possible and expected), this is of little importance. It is light found within human beings, rather than physical light, that must shine resplendently to overcome the darkness.

In these times, when inner circumstances prompt *the reappearance of the Christ* in each human, once again this sublime energy of love finds little receptivity in human hearts. Notwithstanding efforts made by the inner being to place them on the path of truth, how many choose to stray from that path? How many, even knowing that the nourishment for inner life is clearly expressed in the affirmation of Christ: "My food is to do the will of the One who sent me and to complete His work..." (John 4:34), want to enter this life while still holding on to worldly pleasures?

Currently we are living through times in which the inner essence of many beings pleads to surrender to deeper realities: "I came from the Father and have come into the world and now I leave the world to go to the Father." (John 16:28) Nevertheless, the

---

[16] **Primeval triad.** Original trinity that expresses the energies of Will (the Father), of Love (the Son) and of the Light (the Holy Spirit).

greater part of humanity turns away from the light of wisdom, thus widening the external disparities and contributing to degradation of material life and to primitive and barbaric patterns of human behavior. Those who can truly understand what is happening in the world today turn inward and dedicate themselves to a silent work of restoring balance to planetary life. Those who give in to the forces of degeneration confirm their destination: they will be taken to lower stages of evolution. The same Love that granted them their lives offers them an opportunity to begin their evolutionary journey again.

Even before all the retrievable portion of humanity and of the other kingdoms is rescued, which does not necessarily mean immediately leaving the material level, the darkening of the three worlds of human life (mental, emotional and physical-etheric) will be intensified. When the rescue is completed, a global purification will take place.

✧ ✧ ✧

Fifth stage – the final moments on Golgotha: the inevitable reaction

The veil of the temple is torn in two, from top to bottom;
the earth trembles, rocks are split,
tombs open and many righteous come back to life.

"I tell you most solemnly, the hour will come — in fact it is here already — when the dead will hear the voice of the Son of God, and all who hear it will live." (John 5:25) It is a well-known fact that, unless individuals are aware of inner realities, their life contributes little toward evolution. They are considered dead since they have not yet entered into the real Life. However, if they hear and answer the call, humans awaken to this Life and are born spiritually.

The fact that the crucifixion of Christ-Jesus took place on Golgotha, which means "the place of the skull," holds a hidden symbolism related to the current process of transition, since the greatest conflict among the forces that are impervious to light takes place on the mental level.

At any moment in the current period of transition, planetary chaos can become widespread. Every minute in the operation of a nuclear power plant is a risk to all the Earth, increasing the threat of continual and widespread pollution of the soil, water and air.

Therefore, the retribution that the law of karma will bring upon humanity to balance its criminal acts, is irrevocable. The time is coming when the last drop will cause this chalice filled with violence against planetary life to overflow. In re-balancing, the forces of Nature, governed by elevated consciousnesses, will act in a powerful way. Each individual will receive a measure of this retribution according to what he or she has done, since the law of material karma is rigorous and just.

When the retrievable portion of the kingdoms of the planet has been rescued, the purification and transmutation process on the material levels will be intensified. The confrontation between light and darkness will become even more intense; "...there will be great distress such as, until now, since the world began, there has never been..." (Matthew 24:21). The outcome of this battle has been decided — light will prevail. It is only a matter of time for certain events to take place in the world of forms.

During this period, beings who had served the Hierarchy on

the surface of Earth in the past and who are prepared to respond effectively to the commands of the inner regency of the planet under difficult external circumstances, will once again be working on material levels. They will often transcend the law of birth through monadic transmutation[17] and become present on these levels.

✧ ✧ ✧

Sixth stage – the burial: a new opportunity for those who remained silent

Joseph of Arimathaea, eminent member of the council that condemned Jesus but who does not agree with the decision, takes it upon himself to bury the body of Jesus in a new tomb.

The pure and the innocent who knew how to keep their light shining, do not fear nightfall. Even in darkness they are able to find the Path. They will scarcely see or become affected by the most crucial moments of the planetary transition when conflict and chaos will devastate the surface of the Earth. They will have understood and followed the words of Christ: "...anyone who drinks the water that I shall give will never be thirsty again: the water that I shall give will turn into a spring inside of him, welling up to eternal Life." (John 4:14)

---

[17] **Transmutation.** On the material level, the raising of the energy potential on the mental, emotional and physical-etheric level of existence or, on the monadic level, the withdrawal of a monad from its material bodies, yielding them to a more evolved monad. Through transmutation, the monad that hands over the bodies frees itself from the law of physical death.

There are also those who will not be spared from participating in the final moments since they had not acted upon their choice for the life of the Spirit as fully as they could have. These beings were called and they heard and intended to respond, but they did not follow through. They will still have another opportunity to offer themselves to evolutionary service during those times of extreme need. They, too, will reach their destiny of peace, for once a lamp is lit, it goes on radiating its brightness.

In order for certain processes of purification, transmutation and transubstantiation[18] to occur in the current constitution of planetary matter, they must be totally shielded from human influence. These processes, such as the implantation of the new genetic code, GNA,[19] and the seeding of new organs in the physical body, take place silently within beings and are only revealed when they are relatively complete. During the present transition, intergalactic consciousnesses are also carrying out these processes on the rescuable portion of the planet's population. Although these processes take place far from the eyes of the world, they are aided by devoted servers, members of humanity of the surface.

✧ ✧ ✧

The priests send guards
to keep watch over the tomb.

The greater part of the forces of involution will be ousted from the planet during the present planetary transition. The

---

[18] **Transubstantiation.** The occult process of liberation of inner energy immanent in all manifested life. Through transubstantiation, particles elevate their vibration to a higher level.

[19] **GNA.** This acronym denotes an electromagnetic field, not a specific chemical substance.

extent to which evil forces are present on a planet depends on the evolution of the Logos that rules it and this is reflected in the humanity that inhabits the planet.

The Earth, as a consciousness, is undergoing the Fourth Cosmic Initiation. Compared to the Initiations lived by human beings, we know that at this point the Earth is acquiring control over the material forces of the densest sublevels. This control will only be consummated in the Fifth Initiation.

Depending on the level of the Earth's evolution, in the coming stage its inhabitants may still be involved with dark forces. Humanity, as a whole, will have reached the First Initiation. In accordance with the laws, especially the law of magnetic attraction, such forces will naturally continue to be drawn to the earthly environs until humans free themselves completely from these dark forces.

Nevertheless, the current processes of purification, transmutation and transubstantiation are preparing for the birth of a new Earth that will respond to the designs of the intergalactic councils.[20] Today's human mind cannot even imagine the magnitude and the beauty of the coming stage. While these processes occur in a veiled manner within the core of beings and in the very substance of the material levels of consciousness, the forces of involution watch but cannot intervene.

---

[20] **Councils.** Groups of elevated consciousnesses that guide evolution within a given sphere. A council is an extension of the central regency within that ambit, a support nucleus for the manifestation of the purpose of the regency.

Seventh stage – the resurrection: the new times are prefigured

> *Three days go by after the burial;*
> *Mary Magdalene and some other women go to the tomb*
> *where Jesus has been laid and find it open;*
> *an angel tells them that Jesus has come back to life.*

Very few people have understood the assertion: "...if you do not eat the flesh of the Son of Man and drink his blood, you will not have life in you." (John 6:53) With the incarnation of Christ two thousand years ago, the energy of cosmic love, or cristic energy, permeated the material spheres to their densest levels. This greatly increased the capacity of life on the surface of the Earth to respond to cosmic and solar impulses. If it had not been for the incarnation of Christ, the planet would not have been able to continue on its evolutionary path.

Jesus addressed the following words to the portion of humanity that resisted contact with higher impulses: "I have come in the name of my Father and you refuse to accept me." (John 5:43) To those who willingly accepted these impulses, he said: "...that Spirit of Truth whom the world can never receive since it neither sees nor knows him; but you know him, because he is with you..." (John 14:17)

During the present planetary transition, cristic energy is again permeating the planet in a special way. It will arise more clearly than it has ever done before, as was announced: "...for as the lightning flashing from one part of heaven lights up the other, so will be the Son of Man when his day comes." (Luke 17:24)

New life can already be perceived by many rescuable beings

on the planet. It is characterized by feminine energy[21] and by closer contact with the creator-angels. The day is coming when there will be more light in the sky and when the sky will become more than a firmament. The horizons will then have been lifted and humanity will have crossed through the veils that separate it from true life. However, before this stage of greater clarity can exist on the surface of the planet, the cycle of transition, including phases of purification and harmonization, will have to be completed.

✧ ✧ ✧

> *Jesus appears to Mary Magdalene revealing to her that he was ascending to the Father.*

In the coming reharmonization of the planet, which will have the support of spiritual and divine hosts, the densest portion of the Earth's karma with the solar system and the cosmos will be balanced. Humanity will have to be prepared to undergo this intense reharmonization. The destination of each being has already been determined; the choices have been made and no matter which path is taken, it will be under the protection of infinite cosmic love. As Christ said: "Do not let your heart be troubled. Trust in God still, and trust in me. There are many rooms in my Father's house; if there were not, I should have told you. I am going now to prepare a place for you, and after I have gone and prepared you a place, I shall return to take you with me; so that where I am you may be too." (John 14:1-3)

The children of the new Earth will be able to recognize themselves as children of the Sun. The boundaries that previously

---

[21] **Feminine energy.** Energy in itself is neutral, but when manifested in cosmic physical life it can take on a receptive (feminine) or a creative (masculine) quality. The Earth is currently entering into a phase in which its evolutionary processes will be characterized by feminine energy.

kept them within planetary limits will be extended as far as solar life.

✦ ✦ ✦

The Future

When the redemption of the planet has been more completely accomplished, it will allow humanity to live a harmonious existence of peace and service to the Creator. Traces of its conflictive past will be few compared to the abundance that will be lived. The balms of love and life that the One Source will pour over the Earth from now on will heal the traumas of the dark times.

> A woman in childbirth suffers because her time has come, but when she has given birth to the child she forgets the suffering in her joy… (John 16:21)

✦ ✦ ✦

Future humanity will no longer appear to be a cluster of irreconcilable groups that oppose one another, such as it is today. Humans will gradually recognize their unity with the supreme life and devote their energies to it. Silently, the inner being of each liberated person will say to his or her brothers and sisters that proceed toward this unification with the Spirit: "You know the way to the place where I am going." (John 14:4)

✦ ✦ ✦

Chronological time does not exist above the mental level. Therefore, if we attain supra-mental life, it is possible to live this new world today. For this to happen Christ touched the hearts of those who were willing to become the seeds of the new life. He addressed the Father, saying: "As you sent me into the world, I have sent them into the world, and for their sake I consecrate myself so that they too may be consecrated in truth." (John 17:18-19)

✧ ✧ ✧

The field is ready. The seeds have been sown. All they need is to be nurtured.

A light within each being endeavors to become manifested. Created in the image of The One Who sustains the universes, it is transcendent and immanent. It is hidden beneath the veils of illusion. However, its inherent qualities allow it to become revealed in matter through each pure expression of the spirit. It is projected even in the form of the rocks that mirror perfection.

The times are coming in which the destiny that human beings have sealed with their choices will be fulfilled. Material life endures states of turbulence due to the conflict that has overtaken the entire planet. In every particle that remains in darkness, the new clashes with the obsolete, the good collides with the bad.

Signs are present in the soil, in the air, in the water, in the wind and in the leaves of the plants that are still attempting to turn toward the Light.

Humanity was cautioned, but did not want to listen; it was warned, but did not want to follow the signs.

What do humans have to say about humanity itself?

✧ ✧ ✧

Doors are being opened revealing far-off frontiers that will also be traversed some day. The flame of life that blazes in the center of this solar system sustains and increases its radiance that vivifies earthly existence. Sparks of love from the heart of the Father ignite everything they touch, immersing the universe in an infinite light.

A dawn of ineffable beauty flares across the sky of the Earth. Words are inadequate to convey the fact that eternity is drawing close to the infinitesimal consciousness of humans.

> *In past times the Children of the Sun arrived on this planet. They came in chariots of fire; they lived among the people of the Earth; in chariots of fire, they returned to their sublime Kingdom.*
>
> *They left teachings, seeds of a more luminous life. However, humanity did not understand them.*
>
> *Today they return, bringing with them the Children of the Flaming Stars and the Children of Blessedness.*
>
> *Sacred are the times that foretell the new School. Blessed are those born of the Celestial Arc who were ready to die to matter; they will be absorbed into the light of eternity and will never again leave it.*
>
> *Many of those from the remote past who were lost in darkness, today walk in the light. This Earth, even in sin and in wickedness, gave gifts to the Heavens. It sheltered those who descended into the abyss and those who were lifted out of the abyss.*
>
> *New times define this Time; new lights anticipate the Great Light. Promises from the Heavens made to humankind are being fulfilled today.*

Part 2

Initiations in the Present Planetary Transition

Occult Aspects of the Initiations

The Initiations of Christ and of Jesus

Initiations are specific processes of expansion of consciousness. They are reflected within the entire energy structure of the being who experiences them, in a way that is inaccessible to the rational mind. To help one become attuned with this path that someday all humans are to tread, some symbols may be used to trace these clearly delineated stages of inner development.

The evolutionary work that is taking place on the planet through elevated consciousnesses, such as Avatars,[1] Entities[2] and

---

[1] **Avatar.** A consciousness freed from compulsory manifestation in the material worlds. When incarnated in service to the Central Government of the Cosmos, an Avatar expresses one of the three divine aspects as fully as possible for that cycle.

[2] **Entity**. An energy vortex of pure life-consciousness that holds the purpose to be fulfilled on a certain sphere in the universe where it is active. Consciousnesses of different vibratory gradations gather and work as extensions of an Entity to accomplish the purpose entrusted to it. An Intergalactic Council, a group of monads or even the inner nucleus of an incarnated group serving the Plan of Evolution, can be considered Entities.

Logoi,³ is an unlimited source of teaching. In many cases, this work is directly linked to the process of Initiation of the human kingdom. Furthermore, manifestations of these consciousnesses on the surface of the Earth indicate that all planetary life is entering higher energy levels; this in turn, prepares for or reflects the Initiations of the Logos of the Planet.

The spiritual teachings transmitted by the Tibetan Master D.K.⁴ in the middle of the twentieth century show that some passages narrated in the Gospels symbolize the Initiations that take place in the human kingdom. Five of these were expressed by Master Jesus, the First to the Fifth Initiation, and five by Christ, the Second to the Seventh Initiation (which was combined with the Sixth). However, one cannot surmise that Christ and Jesus had undergone these Initiations only at the time of living these events. Symbolism in the Gospels seeks to bring students closer to abstract and inner realities.

Christ worked through his disciple, Jesus, during three years and the interaction between these consciousnesses has not yet been fully revealed to humanity. Even though the Christ-Entity had permeated the bodies of Jesus during the baptism in the River Jordan, the complete taking over of the bodies only occurred, in a mysterious way, in the final moments lived on Calvary.

When beings stand on the threshold of divine fulfillment, they must incarnate in order for their encounter with the Source of the flaming life to be consummated and for the remaining tenuous ties with earthly existence to be burnt up in the fiery heat of

---

³ **Logoi.** Nuclei of cosmic consciousness that hold the keys to the manifestation of the universes. Each planet, solar system or galaxy has the origin and the end of its existence in its Logos. The Logos is the life, the rhythmic flow and the sustenance of its universe and of all the particles that constitute it. A Logos reflects the mystery of the primeval triad and can operate concurrently in different points of the cosmos.

⁴ **D.K.** Djwhal Khul. A certain phase of his teachings is contained in the works of Alice A. Bailey.

this Source. The energy produced by this act of letting go is poured over the planet like a balm of healing, renewal and peace.

In a specific incarnation, a being may be given the opportunity to concisely recall past accomplishments and to anticipate future ones. D.K. clarified that the Jesus-being had actually lived his Third Initiation as the biblical figure, Joshua. During his incarnation as Jesus, this being lived two great sacrifices: the giving up of his body to be used by Christ, and the *great renunciation* that characterizes the Fourth Initiation. He attained the Fifth Initiation later when he incarnated as Apollonius of Tyana. Moreover, while Jesus was undergoing several expansions of consciousness that took him to the Fourth Initiation, symbolized by the crucifixion, Christ was experiencing the culmination of the Sixth Initiation and preparing for the subsequent one.

Cristic energy permeated the Jesus-being and, to a lesser degree, the Apostles as well. The Apostles were able to heal and to cast out forces of involution from the auras of other beings even while Jesus was incarnated. Though cristic energy was continuously present in Jesus, the manifestation of Christ through him occurred only at specific times. Christ did not remain within the material bodies of Jesus for any length of time. In this way the evolution and the service of the two beings took place concurrently by means of the same vehicles: the Jesus-being represented the link between humanity and the planetary Hierarchies, and the Christ-being represented the link between the planetary Hierarchies and the solar Hierarchies. The events of the life of Jesus that are partially described in the Gospels may be seen in this light, revealing how the actions of these two beings occurred at the same time during the three years of this experience.

By means of the interaction of the Christ-being and the Jesus-being a seed was planted in the aura of the planet. In the coming stage, this seed will become a mature plant and will bear fruit. This seed bears within it the possibility for monads to incarnate without having to go through physical birth and without the incarnated being who receives the monad having to leave the bodies in order to undergo monadic transmutation. In this way, the vehicles of that incarnated being are also used by another monad that becomes manifested only for the length of time needed to accomplish the sublime work entrusted to it on the material planes. This process, however, must not be mistaken for, or compared with, what happens today when discarnate beings become incorporated in persons who are willing to let this happen. Such incorporations are aberrations in the development of humanity and are contrary to the underlying purpose of the Plan of Evolution. They are vestiges of deviations that occurred in the Atlantean period. The sublime interaction between Christ and Jesus holds the keys to a being's unification with the essence of life, the Father. This is a point of reference for today's student.

Cristic energy is immanent in the life of this solar system. Cristic energy is evolving and by the end of this systemic cycle it should have achieved its perfect expression on all levels of consciousness. Two thousand years ago this energy was already fully present in the Jesus-being to the degree that was possible to be expressed by an incarnated being on the surface of the Earth. But the manifestation of Christ, which occurred simultaneously through the bodies of Jesus, transcended this situation.

The interaction between Christ and Jesus hides realities that so far have only been revealed on the inner levels and to certain Initiates. Today, however, with the energy brought by the planetary transition and with the consummation of the stage that was started two thousand years ago, many veils are being torn away. Humanity can draw near to the Hierarchy in a way that is unprecedented in the history of the Earth.

When Christ incarnated using the bodies of Jesus, a cosmic,

solar and planetary condition came about: the alignment between Sirius, the Sun of this solar system, Venus and the Earth. The planet was able to enter a new stage as a result of the inner achievement reached by Jesus and by Christ. Christ represented the link of the Earth with the Sun and the Brotherhood of Sirius, and Jesus represented the link of the Earth with the Sun through the intermediation of Venus.[5] The Earth-Venus-Sun-Sirius energy circuit was able to be reinforced through the unification of the consciousness of these two beings and the service that they rendered through terrestrial matter (the bodies of the Jesus-being). The wellspring of energies that flowed through Christ in that special conjuncture was not only of a solar level, but also of a cosmic level that issued from Sirius. The power of the cristic manifestation, delicately and patiently prepared throughout the ages by the Hierarchies and by many other manifestations that had previously expressed cristic energy at lower voltages, is concentrated in this event.

> Yes, God loved the world so much that he gave his only Son, so that everyone who believes in him may not be lost but may have eternal life. For God sent his Son into the world not to condemn the world, but so that through him the world might be saved. (John 3:16)

God (Life, Sirius) sent his Son (Love-Wisdom, Sun) to the world (matter, Earth) so that the world could be saved, that is, to liberate the planet from the yoke of the forces of involution and to introduce humanity into eternal life, into the higher laws of evolution.

✧ ✧ ✧

---

[5] **Intermediation of Venus.** Paul Brunton, philosopher, teacher and author, also confirmed the profound link between Master Jesus and Venus.

The Occult Meaning of the Renunciation of Christ and of Jesus

The negative attitude of the great majority of humans of the surface of the Earth in regard to the cyclic opportunity that they were being offered, curtailed their evolution. However, the fact that the Jesus-being reached the Fourth Initiation at the same time that Christ attained the Sixth Initiation, permitted the Earth to leave the necessary and foreseen preparatory stage and to move toward the transition that is currently taking place, thus making the salvation of the planet possible.

In the past, someone who attained the Second Initiation would begin to gain a deeper understanding of renunciation of the world of forms, a process that in this phase occurred mainly on the earthly astral level. In the Fourth Initiation a being learned to renounce the world of souls, allowing the essence of its causal body to be absorbed by the fire of the spirit at a higher level of consciousness. This event is linked to what is esoterically called the *great renunciation*. In the Sixth Initiation the *supreme renunciation* occurs, determining a being's cosmic path and fully taking on the purpose emanated by the Regent-Avatar[6] and safeguarded by the monad. This purpose holds the keys to the being's relationship with the planetary Logos, the solar Logos and the One of Whom nothing can be said. The above description of the Second, Fourth and Sixth Initiations is commensurate with the processes of expansion of consciousness during the past stage of the Earth

---

[6] **Regent-Avatar.** A central nucleus of the being. The Regent-Avatar is the divine spark, the real and eternal pilgrim. It is expressed during its evolutionary path by means of twelve prolongations: seven monads, which are conduits of contact with the manifested universe, and five Principles that interconnect with the non-manifested universe.

when these events were lived by Christ and by Jesus.

Therefore, the energy of Christ was joined to that of the Jesus-being from the time of the baptism in the River Jordan until the *great renunciation* in Gethsemane; however, it was not fully incarnated in his material bodies. With the *great renunciation* the fulfillment of the cosmic will for the Earth was reconfirmed in a way incomprehensible to ordinary people, as expressed in the words, "…your will be done!" (Matthew 26:42)

In this way, what happened in Gethsemane and in the crucifixion should be seen as part of a single event that took place on levels that transcend time and space. In Gethsemane, Christ accomplished the *supreme renunciation*, consummated at the time the Christ-Jesus consciousness abandoned the material bodies when he 'died.' In Gethsemane, within the aura of Christ, Jesus prepared for the *great renunciation*, which was fulfilled through the crucifixion and 'death' on the cross.

Through the 'death' of Christ and of Jesus, occurring under these circumstances, planetary matter was being prepared on the level of ordinary evolution for all of humanity to receive the possibility of transcending the law of death and the law of physical birth. This will be available to many beings in the coming stage of the Earth and to a certain degree it already exists in the present transition. One should not compare the death of an ordinary person with the 'death' of Jesus or relate the 'death' of Jesus to that of Christ. These are three specific stages of evolution that can be represented by three specific situations: a blind person contemplating dawn, someone who sees this dawn and receives its warmth and light, and someone who has become unified with the essence of the light. Thus, the emotional expressions, for centuries cultivated around the suffering lived by Christ-Jesus in the Passion, do not portray reality. Under veils, reality safeguards the glory of planetary redemption.

At the moment of 'death' on the cross, the evolutionary impulses radiated to planetary life in past cycles, many of which were reenacted in the life of Jesus, merged with the evolutionary impulse of the future stage. This fusion was expressed in the tearing away of a veil on the inner levels of existence.

And at that, the veil of the Temple was torn in two from top to bottom; the earth quaked. (Matthew 27:51)

Christ concurrently attained the Sixth Initiation and part of the Seventh. Through that experience, he was able to consummate the stages of the Seventh Initiation that were related to material levels. This process has been unfolding throughout these last two thousand years and will culminate with *the reappearance of the Christ* within each being.

Christ could only approach the bodies of Jesus more intensely in the three-dimensional world after Jesus had undergone the *great renunciation*. By imprinting the energy of renunciation on the matter of the entire planet, Master Jesus could prepare this matter to be taken on by Christ, an act that would be consummated two thousand years later. Furthermore, cosmic circumstances determined that the Initiations of these two beings should occur exactly in this way. Thus, a channel linking the material levels with logoic will was opened by means of the energy of renunciation intensely radiated there: the *great renunciation* expressed by Jesus and the *supreme renunciation* expressed by Christ.

In the past, the energy of sacrifice, recognized in a special way in the Fourth Initiation, was revealed in still greater depth when a being reached the Sixth Initiation. Having decided its cosmic path, a being came face to face in a unique way with the purpose of the Logos of the Earth and the great sacrifice incurred by the Logos in taking on the manifestation of this planet. It was necessary for both the disciple Jesus and Christ to undergo 'death' at the culmination of the crucifixion. The giving of cristic energy to those who had accepted its light, and also to those who did not understand it, had to be imprinted on the life of the surface with the potency of an Avatar and not only that of a Master.

The total incarnation of Christ into human mental, emotional and physical-etheric bodies could not last more than a few hours, even though these bodies had been carefully prepared for centuries. The final phase of the transmutation of the Jesus-being that made this incarnation possible, began with the renunciation expressed in the garden of Gethsemane.

The hidden nuances of this process are inaccessible to the analytical mind. To grasp something of this immeasurable wellspring of grace and renewal of planetary life, one must bear in mind that existence takes place concurrently on the different levels of consciousness. One must abstain from human inferences about these realities that no longer pertain to the human kingdom but to the infinite kingdom of the spirit. In this way it is easier to understand that at certain times the same event was lived in different ways by two beings 'incarnated' in the same bodies. The laws that normally govern evolution on the Earth were not in effect during this event; other laws, under the blessing of the Brotherhood of Sirius, were descending to the planet.

> ... I tell you most solemnly, you will see heaven laid open and above the Son of Man, the angels of God ascending and descending. (John 1:51)

Thus, the Jesus-being attained the Fourth Initiation in the crucifixion. At the same time, the Sixth Initiation was consummated in the Christ-being. In an occult way, the 4 (Fourth Initiation of Jesus) was added to the 6 (Sixth Initiation of Christ) amounting to 10, the number of the Perfect Human, the expression of the Creator-Divinity of the universes, a being's path of fulfillment in cosmic unity.

The impulse sent to the Earth two thousand years ago will complete its cycle of activity in the present planetary transition. The process of Initiation itself is also undergoing transition. This transition will last until Initiations become established in accordance with a future energy structure, when the vibratory pattern of the entire planet will be different. By then, the field of action of the forces of involution will have been reduced to a minimum and the new genetic code will have been implanted in the humanity that will inhabit the surface of the Earth. United with the Hierarchy, humans will then more easily be able to perceive, act upon and accomplish the supreme designs of the Logos of the Earth.

Signs of the present planetary transition are evident in all that is happening today and humans are being given opportunities for growth that are inaccessible in so-called normal times. Those who draw near to the Portals of the Inner Temple with sincerity, purity of intention and humility, and who aspire to surrender themselves exclusively to inner life and serve that life only, are permeated by the Grace that allows them to advance quickly on the *Path of Revelation*.

According to the law of material karma, all actions set in motion a reaction in order to reach equilibrium. This law acts on the material levels of the universes. It reflects aspects of the law of magnetic attraction on the dense levels of existence and, like all laws, it is derived from the one law. Therefore, sincere surrender to inner life attracts a response from sublime nuclei. Those beings who truly allow themselves to be guided by the wisdom of the spirit are drawn to this inner life. The Source of life builds the pathway for each of its children to return to the cosmic Dwelling Place with the same care, beauty and perfection that it manifests in each dawn.

Initiations Today

Preliminary Considerations

Initiations permit an individual to use the three fundamental energies that make possible the manifestation of life and matter on the various levels of existence in the universe: fire by friction, electric fire, and cosmic fire (see diagram on page 70).

Fire by friction characterizes the entire cosmic physical level but is primarily manifested on its material sublevels. It is the principal energy expressed in the constructive and destructive processes that take place in the densest spheres of earthly existence (mental, emotional and physical-etheric). It is the result of the contact of subtle energies (electric and cosmic fires) with concrete matter. Fire by friction is basically expressed through attrition.

When it expresses its higher vibration, fire by friction, immanent in mental substance, gives rise to an illuminating spark, a reflection of the light from the body of the soul. This spark makes it possible for the mind to recognize the idea that represents the purpose of the being's life in that stage of development. It allows one to build a thought-image of this idea and to plan outer life in accordance with this image.

Fires	Levels of Consciousness			Nuclei of Consciousness of the Being
Cosmic Fire	Cosmic, astral, mental, and other higher levels	Non-material levels	Sublime levels	
	Cosmic physical level	1. Divine	Abstract levels	Regent
		2. Monadic		Monad
Electric Fire		3. Spiritual		Body of Light
		4. Intuitive		Soul / Causal Body
		5. Abstract mental / Concrete mental		
Fire by Friction		6. Astral (emotional)	Material (or concrete) levels	Ego (mental, emotional and physical-etheric bodies)
		7. Etheric / Concrete physical		

The three fundamental energies in relation
to levels of existence and nuclei of consciousness of the being

On the emotional level, the higher expression of fire by friction stimulates the emergence of what could be called "energy vortices of aggregation." Upon receiving the stimulus of more potent fires, a being responds on an emotional level through fire by friction. Thus stimulated, this fire brings forth these vortices of pure and elevated desire that attract the energy of the desired object to their center.

The importance of controlling one's thoughts has been disseminated widely in the Teachings during past decades. However, students do not always realize that thought is symbolically like the spark that starts up an automobile, and that an automobile cannot run without fuel (the world of emotion). In this analogy, the movement of the automobile represents the action of the person and the motor represents that which shapes external forms. One can see that the fuel must be free of impurities for the automobile to run as it should and for the motor to function correctly.

This spark, which comes from the stimulation of fire by friction on the mental level, has within it the power to propel the other lower bodies to act according to the direction given by the mind. In these times, people's attention ought to be focused on levels that are higher than the mental level, because by remaining in this more subtle attunement, the mind will establish a higher quality of vibration.

The energy of life on the intuitive and spiritual levels is characterized by electric fire. Its basic qualities are polarity and the harmonious interaction of opposing currents, creating a field of tension that permits the light to come forth.

Cosmic fire is the energy that characterizes the monadic and divine levels. Its essence is expressed mainly through emanation on the supra-human level.

The Process of Initiation in the Present Transition

In the first three Initiations, the soul draws closer to the being's material bodies. These Initiations are a preparation for matter to be permeated by inner energy and to be freely expressed on concrete levels, and in this way be redeemed. For this to happen, the being's nuclei of consciousness on the spiritual, intuitive and causal levels must have already acquired a certain alignment with the monad, otherwise, the monadic impulse cannot reach dense matter since it does not have an adequate channel for its transmission.

Up to the present time, control and alignment of the mental, emotional and physical-etheric bodies, and their alignment with the soul, have required much dedication, perseverance and effort during an individual's many lifetimes. By putting aside negative emotional reactions and unkindly acts, one begins to take on inner and outer attitudes in keeping with spiritual patterns. In the early stage one is able to curb disharmonious actions but one still does not have control over the astral emanations, much less mental ones, such as thoughts of anger or antagonism that act on subtle levels even when they are not externalized. In the later stage, one would already be able to control one's emotions and, eventually, one's thoughts as well.

The first three Initiations can basically be understood as stages in which one is given control of actions, feelings and thoughts. In this case the ego no longer directs the human forces, but the soul begins to prevail. By means of these Initiations one reaches a state in which one becomes master of one's material bodies. However, the bodies retain reactions and resistance (although these gradually diminish) until one crosses the Portal of the Fifth Initiation.

The following reflections highlight some basic aspects of the seven Initiations today.

The First Initiation

The First Initiation works mainly on the relationship of the soul to the consciousness of the physical-etheric body. In this Initiation the soul begins to gain greater control over the impulse that gives shape to forms that are stimulated by fire by friction on the physical level. This does not mean that the soul attains total control over fire by friction, but rather that the soul is then given the opportunity to develop this ability.

From an inward perspective, this Initiation corresponds to the beginning of a more precise alignment of the being's nuclei of consciousness, from the monad to the soul. What takes place is analogous to what can be seen when a magnet is placed near iron filings, forming a configuration that follows the circulation of its subtle magnetic currents.

It becomes clear, therefore, that the process of Initiation is always lived on the being's inner levels. If the monad were not ignited and did not reach higher levels of energy potential, it would be unable to stimulate the alignment of the infra-monadic nuclei. This activation of the monad comes as the result of development that occurs on even deeper levels, in the consciousness of the Regent-Avatar.

When necessary, the monad can receive the help of external intermediaries having elevated consciousnesses, to stimulate a being on its various levels and to activate the circulation of its energy. Ever since Atlantean times the process of Initiation on Earth has required such help.

The First Initiation brings a greater alignment of a being's inner nuclei of consciousness with the monad. When mirrored as light of the soul, monadic energy permeates the three permanent atoms[7] and in a particular way, the physical permanent atom, that begins to raise its vibration. Thus, stimulated by the soul, the energy of the physical-etheric level begins to intermingle with the energy of more subtle levels.

This stimulation, brought on by the light of the soul, increases progressively throughout the first three Initiations. It begins on the densest level and gradually becomes more subtle. The physical permanent atom is the most materialized of the three and has the slowest vibration, therefore it is the first to resonate with this energy. When this resonance between the physical permanent atom and the light radiated by the soul occurs, it begins to vibrate on higher sublevels and is gradually transformed until it reaches the highest strata of the physical level. There it will await the total absorption of its essence into the center of the being.

Therefore, in the First Initiation the being recognizes its inner group as it becomes integrated into a new level of Hierarchy. It will then penetrate deeper and deeper into its inner group until it reaches the Third Initiation, at which point it will also have greater access to the other inner groups active on the planet.

The Second Initiation

This Initiation is attained by overcoming many struggles, since it is directly related to the astral level of the Earth. While the First Initiation is like plunging into a great ocean of consciousness, the path to reach the Second can be seen as the struggle of a ship-

---

[7] **Permanent atoms.** Seed-atoms, the synthesis of all the experiences of a being on the material levels from the time it entered the human kingdom. Each one of the bodies of the being on those levels has a permanent atom.

wrecked person in the whirlpools of the most dangerous waters of this ocean. However, these struggles are necessary for the being to gain control over these waters and find calmer seas.

The trials of this stage are experienced intensely by the Initiate since these processes reflect on the astral body, which by nature tends to exacerbate its reactions. Harmony and balance are two of the goals of this Initiation, which can be viewed as a deep cleansing, normally requiring more than one incarnation to be accomplished. However, in times of opportunity such as today, one can go through many stages in a single lifetime.

When the energy of the soul attains greater power and is able to permeate the astral sublevels, making the substance of these sublevels vibrate in harmony with its frequency, the being undergoes a great crisis. This crisis leads to the consummation of the Second Initiation, whereby a resonance is established between the astral permanent atom and the energy of the soul.

A second level Initiate has access to sectors of the inner groups that are withheld from those of the first level. In this stage, the being is more firmly affiliated with the Hierarchy and the links are more consolidated than in the previous Initiation. But only upon attaining the Third Initiation does the individual go beyond the affiliate level to become a part of the Hierarchy.

In this second stage the soul experiences better control over fire by friction, which, on the astral level, is expressed by means of energy vortices that bring about aggregation. The soul is given the opportunity to exercise its capacity to stimulate the manifestation of the Plan of Evolution on the astral level of Earth when it creates pure emanations in the form of elevated desires. Nevertheless, this is guided by higher regencies that are supra-human and is not directed toward the soul itself.

A high level of illusion and glamour still enshrouds humanity of the surface. So, when addressing the subject of Initiations, one must repeatedly underscore that this process is not aimed at the individual's fulfillment on human levels or the confirmation of ideals. Rather, Initiation seeks to merge these levels and all the other levels successively into the core of the being. It is the path to a supra-corporeal life and to contact with nonmaterial realities.

The Third Initiation

In this Initiation the alignment among the spiritual, intuitive and causal levels of a being, which had begun in the First Initiation, is consummated. The ego is now brought under total control by the power of spirit reflected in the inner mirror of the soul. Starting with this 'great crisis', the person begins to manifest more faithfully the impulses sent by the soul on the three human levels. The fusion of the personality with the soul occurs in a definitive way in the Third Initiation. It is a glorious moment in the life of a being and has notable effects on the evolution of all humanity.

It is interesting to perceive the relationship that exists between the Fifth, Third and First Initiations. This alignment begins in the First, is consummated in the Third and is finally absorbed into a channel of direct communication between the spiritual nucleus and the cerebral consciousness in the Fifth Initiation.

An important event is taking place in the present planetary transition that indicates how Initiations will be in the future. In the past the mental permanent atom was not totally permeated by the energy of the spirit until the Fourth Initiation, since it was situated in the first sublevel of the mental abstract level and therefore on the same level as the soul. In the present transition the causal nucleus, the soul, has begun to relocate to the intuitive level. Therefore, in the Third Initiation the vibration of the mental permanent atom can be elevated and be permeated by monadic fire. Thus, the mental permanent atom itself begins to participate in the alignment of the personality. In the past, however, it was the mental nucleus located in the concrete thinking mind that carried out this function. This has become possible due to the fusion of the levels of consciousness and to the elevation of the vibration of the entire planet.

Certain events in the life of Jesus symbolize the Initiations as they used to occur in the past stages of the Earth and they give a glimpse of how they are taking place in the present transition. However, the future process of Initiation will follow archetypal patterns that only now have begun to be reflected with more clarity on the etheric strata of the planet.

The threshold of the Third Initiation is presented in the Gospels through the transfiguration of Jesus in the presence of three apostles.

The Fourth Initiation

The Fourth Initiation holds the keys of a being's redemption that is currently consummated in the Sixth Initiation. In the Fourth Initiation part of the body of the soul is dissolved and the fire of the monad, the jewel at the center of the thousand-petal lotus, then shines resplendently, revealing the glory of the Children of God on the causal level. The essence of the causal body becomes integrated into the body of light, focused on the spiritual or atmic level, and it enhances that body. This phase is part of the preparation for the monad to absorb all of the nuclei below it.

Intimately related to the *Mystery of Sacrifice*, this Initiation permits the being to draw a little closer to cosmic reality by renouncing the world of the soul. The life of the soul and its projection on the three levels of human existence are 'dissolved' as an act of praise to higher existence. What is vertical is perfectly aligned with what is horizontal and becomes absorbed into the center of the cross formed by these two streams of energy.

All the experiences of the being on the material levels that have been thus far safeguarded by the soul, complete a cycle. This experience is absorbed by the fire that liberates the spirit. The veil that had separated the being's consciousness from the spiritual level is torn away.

The process of Initiation today is undergoing profound transformation, therefore it becomes difficult to chart with precision the experiences that are lived in successive Initiations. This is so because, depending on the monadic potential already awakened and the destiny of the being after the planetary transition, the threshold between one Initiation and another is shifted. Certain phases that would have been part of the subsequent Initiation occur earlier. The process of Initiation is taking place with groups. In this process, an entire group of monads is permeated by a strong energy impulse and under a single vibratory wave each monad takes its step and goes through the portal ahead of it. Knowing this, students must avoid fixed rules and must delve into what, in occult terms, is called the law of necessity. This law, the third vertex of the triangle formed by the law of sacrifice and the law of renunciation, is active and governs the elevation of consciousness of beings in a special way during the present times.

The Fifth Initiation

Currently, in this Initiation the fire of the monad shines brilliantly in the core of the body of light and the being can take part in the Inner Schools.[8] Thus, the web of earthly illusion is totally dismantled and the unveiled logoic reality is disclosed to the Initiate. The Initiate lives the purpose of planetary existence like a flame burning within, learns the first syllable of the sound of the solar Logos, and glimpses the monad's cosmic destiny.

Certain aspects that in the past were part of the Sixth Initiation, today have been incorporated into the Fifth. In this time of transition, when the portals of the planetary environs are being opened and are being aligned with the portals of the solar sphere, many beings, upon reaching the Fifth Initiation, are already deciding their cosmic destiny. They are preparing themselves to follow that pathway.

These changes in the way Initiation takes place became possible due to the transmutation of the Logos of the Earth, as well as the presence and action of various extra-systemic beings and entities in the environs of the planet. However, the words of Christ still hold true: "...but, it is a narrow gate and a hard road that leads to life, and only a few find it." (Matthew 7:14)

The Sixth and Seventh Initiations

>...Who will enter the kingdom of heaven, but the person who does the will of my Father in heaven. (Matthew 7:21)

Today, mysteriously, the Sixth and Seventh Initiations together are incorporating processes that previously were experienced in the Seventh, Eighth and Ninth Initiations.

Currently the thresholds between Initiations can change

---

[8] **Inner Schools.** Fields of service and of inner learning for all of the humanities in this solar system. They act on levels that go from the monadic to the causal. Each of the twelve inner groups of the planet is directly connected to a specific Inner School and is a manifestation of it.

according to the destiny of the being and the level of contact between the monad and the Regent-Avatar. This fact is reflected in the degree to which the monad has already awakened to higher realities. To help our understanding, we could establish a correlation between the process of Initiation in the present planetary transition and the process as it was in the past.

Initiations Today	Initiations in the Past
First Initiation	First Initiation and aspects of the Second
Second Initiation	Second Initiation and aspects of the Third
Third Initiation	Third Initiation and aspects of the Fourth
Fourth Initiation	Fourth Initiation and aspects of the Fifth
Fifth Initiation	Fifth Initiation and aspects of the Sixth
Sixth Initiation	Sixth Initiation and aspects of the Seventh and Eighth
Seventh Initiation	Aspects of the Seventh and Eighth Initiations and the entire Ninth

Correlation between present and past Initiation processes.

In the stage corresponding to the Sixth and the Seventh Initiations, the being is totally liberated from the cosmic physical level and is directly affiliated with the Brotherhood of Sirius. The being openly understands the mystery of cosmic evil and severs its contact with the dark forces that make up what is termed the fraternity of darkness. The path of the being is one of synthesis, that is, the being becomes absorbed into the Regent-Avatar. It is the path of divine life, proceeding toward inanimate evolution.

Initiation	Ray Energy	Quality of Energy	Aspect stimulated in the being
I	Ray VII	Order and ceremonial	Restructuring and elevation of the substance of the physical-etheric level and the substance of the three densest sublevels of the astral (emotional) level, based on their corresponding archetypal pattern, preparing this substance for the fusion of these levels.
II	Ray VI	Devotion and idealism	Restructuring and elevation of the substance of the four highest sublevels of the astral level and of the substance of the three densest sublevels of the mental level, based on their corresponding archetypal pattern, preparing this substance for the fusion of these levels.
III	Ray V	Science that synthesizes	Restructuring and elevation of the substance of the mental level, based on its corresponding archetypal pattern; the three levels of the personality blend with the energy of the soul that is already becoming focused on the intuitive level.
IV	Ray IV	Harmony	Elevation of the causal essence and its absorption by the fire of Spirit, which in this phase is focused in the body of light.
V	Rays III and II	Love through service	Tearing away of the tenuous veils that still separate consciousness from the essential reality of planetary existence; choice of a being's cosmic pathway.
VI	Rays II and I	Synthesis and power through love	Revelation of the origins of cosmic evil present on this planet and in this solar system; redemption.
VII	Ray II (Synthesizes the other six Rays)	Love-Wisdom	Total liberation from the cosmic physical level; elevation of the Regent-Avatar

The process of Initiation in the present planetary transition

One may recall that the boundaries between Initiations can be altered, principally as of the Fifth Initiation, depending on the past, present and future circumstances of the Initiate and the group of monads to which the Initiate belongs. Therefore, the above chart is merely a reference for understanding the broad aspects of how Initiations are occurring today.

✧ ✧ ✧

Initiations and the Etheric Centers of a Being

Contact with inner and nonmaterial realities by means of symbols gives human beings the capacity to build thoughtforms that correspond to abstract life. Thus, the mind is indirectly trained for future tasks.

One's mind links up with images and with ideas that permeate it with the energy underlying the symbol. This occurs, for example, when one receives the information that the Atlantean Race was governed by Varuna, Lord of the Waters, that the Aryan Race is governed by Agni, Lord of Fire, and that the Sixth Race will be governed by Indra, Lord of Air.

The will of the Source of Life and Its purpose for creation must be translated into impulses that are understandable to human beings. It is their task to help build the forms that are denoted by these impulses. This work of construction allows the Face of life to be mirrored in matter. However, it takes on different characteristics on each level of consciousness.

Works on the physical level differ from the development of a virtue or the overcoming of an emotional or mental aspect that hinders one's process of evolution. Thus, each level of consciousness has its own mode of action and one has to learn how to deal with it correctly.

Existence is a wholeness; all of its elements are interconnected. What takes place on one level of consciousness is reflected in the others, for they are parts of the Creator's body of manifestation. Therefore, transformations brought about by the evolution of a being on a specific level can cause equally basic transformations on other levels.

This is one reason why the emphasis on the material bodies (mental, emotional and physical-etheric) is not indicated during this phase of planetary transition. Those who are aware of the oneness of life and of the communion between levels of consciousness and who proceed earnestly in the quest for inner reality, should simply turn to their most subtle and purest nuclei in earnest openness. They should thus attune with the energies that emanate from those centers. This is the path for those who know there is no time to waste in struggle and conflict.

Transformation guided by the more subtle energies of electric and cosmic fires must replace perfection through fire by friction, the method used by most people up to now. The evolution stimulated by electric and cosmic fires takes place mainly by means of magnetic attraction (in the case of electric fire) or by subtle refinement released through activating the potential of the being's cosmic energy (in the case of cosmic fire), rather than by the removal of obstacles by means of friction.

Steady attunement with spiritual life, without the doubts that egotism creates, can raise one to levels of purity and power that are able to destroy bonds with material forces. However, it is a gradual process. One moves forward every time one sincerely and dispassionately surrenders one's life to the inner regent.

Having reached the stage of liberation from the densest ties with material life, a being can intermediate the impulses that the Hierarchy sends to humanity and to the sub-human kingdoms. These impulses are to reach the most rudimentary levels of manifestation. To cooperate in the work of the Hierarchy in this way depends on how far one surrenders to inner guidance.

Those who have already been able to contact the akashic worlds know that all the records from the beginning to the end of Creation can be found there in code. Humanity of the Earth must nurture the capacity for abstraction, the ability to relate to symbols and energies that transcend its crystallized mental mechanisms. This ability emerges with the activation of the pineal gland, which in turn guides the awakening of the pituitary gland.[9] The pineal gland holds the link between material life and inner life. If awakened, the pituitary gland can influence the transformation of the mind, expanding it from rationalism to intuition.

The etheric centers in the human energy system of the chakras in the previous planetary stage are directly related to the glands of the physical body.

Centers (chakras)	Glands / Organs
Head center	Pineal
Ajna center	Pituitary
Throat center	Thyroid
Heart center	Thymus
Solar plexus center	Pancreas
Sacral center	Reproductive organs
Base of the spine center	Suprarenal

Linkages between chakras and glands

---

[9] **Pituitary and pineal glands.** The pituitary gland is directly linked to the integration of the personality; the pineal gland is linked to the fusion of the personality with the soul.

The physical-etheric constitution in humans is undergoing profound change. One sign of change is that the energy system composed of seven chakras is being synthesized into three main centers of right side consciousness (see chart page 86).

In the future constitution of humans, material bodies formed by the GNA will reveal etheric centers that differ from the former system of chakras.[10] The present transition that has made the awakening of the right side consciousness possible, is a stage of energy adjustment and realignment. It is preparing for an etheric system that will function in accordance with new patterns. The fusion of the levels of consciousness has direct consequences for the interrelationship of the human mental, emotional and physical-etheric bodies.

The head energy center, the ajna energy center and the throat energy center are beginning to merge into one, the right side mental center. The human cognitive and creative capacities can then become unified, thus bringing greater equilibrium to one's relationship with outer life. Rational mental activity will gradually move into the subconscious level and become an automatic process, similar to the organs of the physical body today.

In this restructuring of the energy centers of the being, the right side heart center absorbs all of the energy of the chakra heart center as well as part of the energy of the throat center and of the solar plexus center.

When the right side cosmic center (located below the last rib) becomes activated, it draws into itself the energy of the solar plexus center, of the sacral center and of the center at the base of the spine.

In the same way that the energy transmigrated from the

---

[10] See Trigueirinho, *Beyond Karma*, op. cit.

planetary center of Shamballa to that of Miz Tli Tlan,[11] awakening the latter and leading the former into a state of withdrawal, a similar process is taking place with the right side consciousness centers and the chakras. This comes about through the shifting of the energy that vitalized the chakras and not by displacement of the system of chakras itself.

Right side consciousness centers which assimilate the energy of the chakras through their activation	Energy centers of the chakras assimilated into the right side consciousness centers
Right side mental center	Head center Ajna center Throat center
Right side heart center (including parts of the throat center and the solar plexus chakras)	Throat center Heart center Solar plexus center
Right side cosmic center	Solar plexus center Sacral center Base of spine center

Summary of the changes from the chakras to the
right side consciousness centers

The process of Initiation in the past stage of evolution, which ended on 8/8/88 (August 8, 1988), established a relationship between the human and planetary Initiations and the chakras.

---

[11] See Trigueirinho, *Calling Humanity* [Minas Gerais, Brazil: Irdin Editora], page 43.

Initiations in the past stage	Energy centers that are activated
I	Sacral center
II	Solar plexus
III	Ajna center
IV	Heart center
V	Base of the spine center
VI	Throat center
VII	Head Center
VIII	Hierarchy
IX	Shamballa

Relationship between past Initiations and energy centers

In the present period of transition, the energy potential activated by the Hierarchies on the inner levels of planetary life has exceeded what had been planned. The way the foreseen stage was to develop and be manifested on the material levels depended a great deal on humanity's response. This response has been minimal, therefore the Hierarchies have supplemented whatever has been possible under the law.

The link between the Earth and Sirius is occult and it influences the transformation process of the Initiations. The adjustments and changes now taking place are part of the preparation for the coming stage and for the activation of specific energy centers of the great body of the planetary Logos and the solar Logos. These energy centers will begin to vibrate at a new frequency.

Initiations in the human kingdom are merely a fraction of the logoic initiatory process. Each human being who attains an Initiation, thereby reaching a higher level of vibration and radiating the fire and light of this new level, is an atom of the logoic body that has been elevated. The energy circuit of the Logos of the Earth itself is experiencing transformation in the same way that the energy circuits in human beings are now undergoing profound changes with the activation of right side consciousness centers. We have examples of this transformation in the awakening of the receptive feminine polarity of the planet expressed through the intraterrestrial center of Miz Tli Tlan and the manifestation of the new Initiation procedures for the human kingdom.

Initiation in the present phase of transition	Energy center that is activated	Activating fire
I	Right side cosmic center	Fire by friction and electric fire
II	Right side heart center	Fire by friction and electric fire
III	Right side mental center	Fire by friction and electric fire
IV	The three centers of the right side consciousness	Electric fire and cosmic fire
V	The three centers of the right side consciousness	Electric fire and cosmic fire
VI	Monad	Cosmic fire
VII	Regent-Avatar	Cosmic fire

Activating fires in relation to present Initiations and energy centers

Seen in this way, the entire path of the Initiations, from the probationary stages to the stages of final liberation of the being, can be understood in its proper perspective. Initiation is seen in its precise position within the All of which it is a part. Thus it loses the personal connotation that is often imparted to Initiation by the fanciful imagination of the human mind still centered upon itself.

Two thousand years ago Christ announced: "...I have been telling you all this in metaphors, the hour is coming when I shall no longer speak to you in metaphors; but tell you about the Father in plain words." (John 16:25)

Thus, the time was to come when the revelation would be given openly to those of humankind of the surface of the Earth who were seeking and pleading for light. This time has arrived. Truth is revealed in a special way within the intimacy of each being who is open to it. The *Mystery of Sublime Existence* is reflected in the inner mirrors of the planet. In light and glory, it tears away the veils on the surface of the Earth that separate humans from reality.

Part 3

Epilogue

The Cross and Eternity

The Cross and the Path of Initiation

The symbol of the cross is as ancient as humanity itself. Its origin has no definite time or place. It has been present throughout the ages in diverse cultures. Through the cross, human beings have been stimulated to penetrate mysteries that guide them to the essence of life.

According to esoteric teaching, the cross and the tree of life are equivalent symbols. This is emphasized by H.P.B. when stating that the image of a crucified person represents the circumstance into which the Initiate is reborn after crucifixion on the Tree of Life. This 'tree' was exoterically converted into a tree of death because of the way it was used by the Romans as an instrument of torture and because of the ignorance of the first organizers of Christianity.[1]

The cross was, is and will be part of the path of human Initiation. In the mystery schools of Greece, Egypt, India and

---

[1] See Helena P. Blavatsky, *The Secret Doctrine, vol. II,* op. cit., page 560.

Chaldea, among others, it was present as a basis for the rebirth of the new human. The Greek neophytes, who received the name Chrests (man of pain and tribulations), used the sign of the cross ritualistically as an element for drawing near to the energy of Initiation.

The Cross and the Four Elements

Throughout history, the symbol of the cross unfolded into a myriad of forms, each one imbued with its own energy and expressing a nuance of the spiritual truth and light that vivifies this symbol. Each form contains some aspect of the great mystery of life, and always conveys impulses of transcendence, of transmutation and of superseding an achieved state of consciousness in order to enter a more subtle one. Whatever its form may be, the cross expresses the perfect balance and the fusion of four basic forces in the sphere of this universe: the four elements.[2]

> ✧ **Earth.** The element earth can either bind human beings to matter with its emanations, or be the malleable substance with which humans can mold their works.
>
> When in the past it was used for Initiations, the cross was not usually placed vertically in the ground, but rather laid upon the ground so that each of its shafts was equally in contact with the earth without any one of them being

---

[2] **Four Elements.** The material base for the manifestation of life: earth, water, fire and air. The life substance of levels of existence is made up of beings called elementals that manifest these four elements and are on a path of evolution parallel to that of humanity.

more important than the other. In the crucifixion of Christ, the vertical shaft of the cross was embedded in the earth with the other end pointing to the sky, symbolizing the beginning of an evolutionary stage that was to bring these opposites into equilibrium. The laws of crucifixion of an ordinary human do not apply in this case. What happened there was an occult process of transmutation of the material essence, making it possible for a new energy pattern to be installed on the planet.

✧ **Water.** The element water expresses malleability and adaptability. If correctly understood, its energy becomes a balancing factor since it contains healing and purifying aspects. Through this element, certain impulses reach material life so that human beings can carry out purification within themselves. This purification is basic to their 'crucifixion', a more advanced stage in which a deeper transmutation takes place in beings.

✧ **Fire.** The element fire characterizes the current human Race[3] of the surface. As it ignites matter, it liberates the light imprisoned in form. It is the element of redemption. As a symbol of a powerful transforming energy, it sets in motion the process of rebirth of the 'crucified' being. Fire is present in the transformation occurring today on the planet and no individual is untouched by it. For some, contacting this element seems to be a factor of conflict, since its energy removes crystallization, but for those who have taken up the spiritual path, it is a blessing.

---

[3] **Race.** Evolutionary stage specific to the human kingdom, characterized by the development of certain aspects determined by the archetype of humanity. For example, during the manifestation of the Lemurian Race, the physical body and contact with the instinctive level were developed. In the Atlantean race the emotional body and contact of consciousness with the world of desires and feelings were developed. In the current Aryan Race, also called the Fifth Race, the mental body, including the soul, which had been focused on the abstract mental level, was developed and the process of forming links with monadic life was begun.

✧ **Air.** The element air expresses an energy that has a level of vibration closer to that of ether. For this reason, as a vortex, air leads the life of forms to more subtle states. This element has not yet been fully revealed to humanity because it is the next Race, the Sixth, that will be ruled by Indra, Lord of the Air. Nevertheless, air characterizes the intuitive level, to which the causal essence of humans is being drawn. Therefore, in the next stage of the Earth new attributes of the element air will be perceptible to a humanity that will have become more subtle.

The fact that the element air can anchor the energy of the First Ray,[4] that of will-power, for example, is little known today. Yet air has great potential as an instrument for the work of this powerful Ray in dislodging energies and structures, even on the physical levels. This characteristic is present in hurricanes and other natural phenomena caused by the wind. As the sixth sub-Race[5] of the Fifth Race begins to emerge, the activity of the element air is being intensified.

The energies of these four elements gradually become synthesized during the process of Initiation. Humanity should not attempt to control these elements, since such control arises spontaneously when the being awakens to higher levels of consciousness through successive Initiations.

---

[4] **Rays.** Basic energies for the manifestation of life on all levels of existence. Each Ray expresses its nuances and acts on matter according to specific patterns, awakening in it qualities that correspond to its energy. The Second Ray of love-wisdom is characteristic of this solar system and of the Earth.

[5] **Sub-Race.** A race is divided into seven sub-Races, each one maintaining a qualitative relationship with the Race of the corresponding number. In this way, the emerging sixth sub-Race being born (sub-Race of the Fifth Race) has a special link to the future Sixth Race.

Awakening on Higher Levels

In the past, when humans needed a physical material instrument to further their evolution in a certain Initiation, they were tied to a bed in the form of a cross and fell asleep that way. While they slept they went through a kind of 'death' of the involutionary aspects still present in them, thus making it possible for a more subtle energy to emerge and begin to be expressed through them.

The process of Initiation consists of the awakening of the being's consciousness on successively higher levels, symbolically seen as a series of deaths and rebirths.

When the preliminary Initiations (the First and Second) have already been attained, individuals become aware of *Something* that lives within them. They sense the flame of this Life and begin to recognize their oneness with it. They are imbued with reverence because the mark of the Brotherhood of Light is inscribed there. They see that they are not just linked to this Brotherhood, they are actually a part of it, like a drop in an immense ocean, the ocean of the One Life.

Once this flame shines in the Initiates' consciousness, all efforts are directed toward removing anything that obstructs the expression of this inner fire. When renouncing their present state, they gratefully accept the crucifixion of whatever hinders this process.

The *great renunciation*, brought about by the soul, marks the important Fourth Initiation and strengthens the channel of the Hierarchy's contact with humanity.

The renunciation carried out by Christ-Jesus in the garden of

Gethsemane two thousand years ago was not a typical Initiation. What took place there encompassed not only the consciousness of an individual, but the consciousness of the entire planetary Hierarchy and thus it sealed the silent and invisible commitment to redeem material life on the surface of the Earth. This commitment was lived fully by Christ, the present World Teacher, and was taken on by all the Hierarchy of the planet. In this way, matter renouncing itself and surrendering to the will of the spirit began to be activated in a special way by Christ, a cosmic consciousness. Christ imprinted his energy deep within every physical atom in a yet unknown voltage. He brought in the possibility for life of the surface of the Earth to one day become an adequate receptacle for the divine flame.

This 'crucifixion' began two thousand years ago and still goes on today because the process has not yet been consummated. However, this process is reaching its culmination. The Earth will then enter a more luminous stage.

The Three Basic Forms of the Cross

Keys for Change

The expansion of consciousness that humans are undergoing should lead to a more mature relationship with life on all levels of existence. As a result of this expansion, new opportunities to contact more inclusive and subtle realities will arise, taking individuals away from the egocentric focus that prevails today.

Certain keys for this change, transmitted in the past and still valid in the present period of transition, correspond to various stages of human evolution. These keys can be expressed by means of the symbolism of the following three crosses that are related to the evolution of humanity, according to the teachings of D.K.:

✧ the mutable cross or cross of the occult Christ
✧ the fixed cross or cross of the crucified Christ
✧ the cardinal cross or cross of the ascended Christ.

The various forms of the cross express the energies of

different levels of consciousness. The definition of these forms is not random. It is perceived inwardly by Initiates in attunement with archetypal nuclei that govern the evolution of humanity and of the planet.

The Mutable Cross

The mutable cross symbolizes the levels of consciousness going from the level of the ordinary person[6] to that of one who begins the spiritual path.

This cross carries a forceful symbol of the mutability of existence within form. The energy reflected by it rules life of the three-dimensional world, and gives the impulse for purification. It organizes matter, evoking in it a response to light.

However, there is an energy of a more dense vibration that can be associated with this symbol, an energy which leads those who are ambitious along dark paths and turns them away from the truth. It is represented by the figure of the swastika or gammadion cross. The movement of its arms suggests inconstancy, an instability that does not allow the inner light to be revealed. Thus it so well represents "the occult Christ" — the curbing of the manifestation of the inner being's energy.

---

[6] **Ordinary person.** A human being whose consciousness, identified with the life of forms, is eluded by appearances and subject to the natural cycles of evolution.

Nevertheless, the Eastern swastika (see above) expresses the esoteric nature of this symbol more purely. The arms in this form of the mutable cross indicate a counter-clockwise movement that signifies the transcendence of the mental stage because chronological time is a creation of the mind. This cross was used by many peoples in ancient times as a symbol of salvation.[7]

In its pure form this symbol contains an elevated energy that gives humans the impulse to proceed until the time they awaken to the truth and willingly surrender their human nature to crucifixion.

From then on the energy of the fixed cross of Christ crucified shines over humanity.

The Fixed Cross

The fixed cross is the symbol of those who have received the first three Initiations. Under the impulse of inner energy, they surrender to crucifixion and to dieing to matter in order to be spiritually reborn. Therefore, it is the symbol of sacrifice, of giving of the self so that all existence may become sacred.

Those who abide in the energy of this symbol receive its beneficial emanation on the intuitive and divine levels, as well as in

---

[7] **Symbol of salvation.** See Helena P. Blavatsky, *The Secret Doctrine,* op. cit., vol. II, pages 556-557 and 586.

the three dimensional world where they serve the Plan of Evolution.

The transition which the planet is undergoing corresponds to the occult meaning of the fixed cross. For this reason, throughout these two thousand years this form of the cross has been more vitalized and has overshadowed the mutable cross (swastika) that was prominent in the times preceding the cristic coming. H.P.B. stated that the swastika cross is related to the number 6. Based on this, those who are familiar with the monogram of Christ[8] can understand something more regarding the work carried out by the Christ consciousness. This work raised the energy of humanity from the level of the mutable cross to the level of the fixed cross.

Willingness to serve and a sincere effort to fulfill one's part in the Plan of Evolution are inherent to the being who takes up the inner path. Right from the outset of this path one realizes that to be an effective instrument of the Hierarchy one must renounce human nature and silence the impulses of the ego. One perceives that only in this way can one approach the kingdom of cosmic existence and find the necessary energy to collaborate with the Elder Brothers in fulfilling the planetary purpose. The essence of the energy synthesized in the fixed cross contains the mystery of the resurrection.

The image of the fixed cross has been exoterically associated with death but this is a shadowy facet of its symbolism. Those who have answered the inner call can find broader aspects of this symbol within themselves.

One must bear in mind that a symbol is concentrated energy and one must seek the energy itself, otherwise one could run the risk of falling into crystallized forms that would dull the mind and cause it to become more and more dependent on external

---

[8] **The monogram of Christ:** is similar to the cross of six arms.

instruments. The true seeker of the light knows that the path is built on the transcending of structures and that it guides life toward nonmateriality. Therefore, one should be cautious of whatever could limit one's consciousness to forms.

In the past, the symbol of the cross was often used by those preparing for an Initiation as an incentive to ascend. We know that even the sign of the cross adopted by Christian religions and denominations today is an inheritance of old rites of Initiation. However, in those rituals, the use of the sign of the cross by the Initiate was followed by a series of mantras of a high degree of purity, quite different from the chants used today in some religious celebrations.

Experience shows that, especially in the beginning of the path, one must diligently cultivate discipline and external order, providing a practical base for the manifestation of harmony. Later on, discipline and order become a part of life and can be expressed without conscious effort. Aspirants should not confuse negligence with the inner freedom brought by spiritual life. Light cannot shine freely wherever there is disorder and impurity.

The Cardinal Cross

The cardinal cross watches over the path of those who commune with the essence of the Hierarchy. In a special way it expresses the unification of the will of the being with the will of the Source of Life. Therefore it is the cross of the ascended Christ.

The ascending path that leads to the unification of the three aspects of the being (the light of will-power, love-wisdom and intelligent activity) is depicted in this symbol that stimulates integration into cosmic life. The energy of this symbol holds a key to the consciousness of the planet's regent-center.⁹ It also represents the process through which omnipotence is attained by a consciousness that already expresses omnipresence and omniscience.

Through the symbolism of these three crosses, one can grasp some aspects of the interaction of three basic planetary nuclei: humanity, corresponding to the mutable cross; the Hierarchy, represented by the fixed cross; and Miz Tli Tlan, the regent-center of the planet which anchors the energy of the Lord of the World,¹⁰ corresponding to the cardinal cross. Furthermore, these three crosses characterize each of the three fires active in the manifestation of life: fire by friction, electric fire and cosmic fire.

A symbol is the outer vestment of an inner energy. One should strive to contact the energy itself and not simply the form that cloaks the energy. Humanity would take an immense step backward if it were to surrender to the cult of forms in times like these. The deeper one grasps the truth, the more it is revealed divested of coverings.

---

⁹ **Regent-center.** The spiritual regency of the planet is anchored in inner nuclei, which are the intraterrestrial centers that exist on supraphysical levels. One of these centers governs all the others and it is there that the consciousness of the planetary Logos is especially focused. In the current stage, that regent-center is Miz Tli Tlan.

¹⁰ **Lord of the World.** Sublime consciousness, direct channel for radiating the purpose underlying logoic Will to the planetary level.

As humanity mirrors the energy of the mutable cross in the course of its evolution, it should gain control over fire by friction and attain the perfection hidden in the essence of matter. Thus, humanity should guide matter to a high standard of inner organization and receptivity to spiritual light.

Humans should have gained control over fire by friction. If they had attained a reliable level of control, keys to mastery of that fire would have been given to them and today their learning would be taking place in the sphere of electric and cosmic fires. This will only happen globally after the present planetary transition. Nevertheless, there are those who partake in profound realities regardless of what happens in the outer life of the Earth.

The Hierarchy reflects the energy symbolized by the fixed cross, and accomplishes, to a high degree of perfection, the work inherent to electric fire. This energy, fully expressed in the service rendered by the Hierarchy, allows the vitalizing spark of matter to emerge from the harmonious interaction among opposite forces. In the present transition, the Hierarchy penetrates extra-planetary circuits where cosmic fire is the main constructor-element.

The regent-center of the planet corresponds to the energy of the cardinal cross, which mirrors full unity with cosmic life. The consciousnesses that manifest the energy inherent in this symbol have cosmic fire as their instrument of service. These consciousnesses take in other, still higher nonmaterial expressions of fire, as they continue to render service.

The next stage of the Earth will reveal the symbol corresponding to nonmaterial fire. As humanity develops, it will interact with electric fire to a greater degree. This will allow it to use electric fire as an instrument of service and to learn how to contact cosmic fire. In this way, humanity will have totally surpassed the level of the swastika mutable cross and will be able to manifest the energy symbolized by the fixed cross. Humanity of the surface will make important inner connections with planets, stars and constellations, insofar as it attains higher vibratory levels.

The Hierarchy and the regent-center of the Earth will also work with fires that are more potent than the ones today. Therefore, in the coming phase these planetary nuclei will be expressed in other symbols.

The Cross in the Coming Stage of the Earth

Preparing for the Coming Times

Whenever there is a change in the ascending process of planetary life, new symbols are vitalized on the inner levels. The awakened consciousnesses on those levels dedicate themselves to continually radiating the energy contained in those symbols, transmitting them to all who are open to receive them. In this way, the manifestation of future stages is prepared on the subtle levels.

Today many individuals are becoming aware of an inner stimulation of patterns and realities that will only be fully manifested in the coming stage of the planet. This stimulation may even be perceived through symbols, but what really matters is for it to be perceived.

The destiny of all beings is to be united with the supreme nucleus that gives them life. The law that will make it possible is manifested through sublime energies endowed with wisdom and balance. This infinite law is irrevocable.

Nevertheless, an individual who has not found responses to persistent inner urgings in ordinary life could stir up negative attitudes and give in to the forces of dispersal and chaos. It is evident that for New Life to be introduced on Earth, the old structures will have to reach a state of complete destruction. It is also clear that little or nothing of the old structures can be used for the creation of a higher existence. Nevertheless, there is a great difference between commitment to the work of the energies of light and of purification, and involvement with the forces of dispersal that seek to extinguish the flame of life wherever they can.

Those who aspire to prepare the new times should have control over the impulses of involution within themselves. They will then realize that the work of implanting new patterns takes place in different degrees.

Individual Work

Patterns of new life come about to the extent that one fulfills within oneself the same goals to be attained by the outer life of the Earth. On a planetary scale, one individual's isolated action may seem to have little impact. However, when inwardly linked to others who act in consonance with the same aims, this action can move mountains. The contribution of each individual is like the yeast that silently leavens the entire dough.

Group and Planetary Work

When inner groups become externalized and form the base for higher energy to permeate the infra-monadic portion of planetary life, new patterns arise on a group and planetary scales.

The great transformations foreseen for the world are not stimulated by individuals acting alone, but by inner groups that are reflected on the material levels.

Groups in the material world are being activated by the energy coming from inner groups, which draw near to the life of the surface, and by the law of magnetic attraction strongly directed toward the entire Earth. The task of these groups is to mirror subtle realities and to attest to the existence of the inner groups. These inner groups are characterized by well-defined energies. They are governed by highly evolved consciousnesses linked to the planetary Logos, the guiding nucleus of planetary life that works through the Lord of the World.

A group in the material world that is a prolongation of the energy of an inner group emerges from the response given by each being who is to be part of that group. These beings must be free of crystallized mental concepts that stand in the way of their inner truth. A prolongation of such a group is not merely to express human fraternity but to bring about the communion of each being with inner life that holds the essence of this fraternity and the wisdom of true impersonal unity.

These groups on material levels arise from the unification of their members through the energy of a spiritual goal that is known inwardly beforehand by each individual and that gives groups their life and reason for existence.

When there is openness and flexibility in individuals, the external groups that express the energy of the inner groups reflect a pattern of order and harmony above and beyond any merely human accomplishment. They stimulate beings to eliminate what is superfluous and to move toward simplicity, the foundations upon which the truth of the spirit is to be built. These groups unfold from within, from the ardor of the spiritual flame that seeks to be expressed in a seemingly hostile world. When they are formed in this way, and hold fast to the purity of their inner origin, they come close to the consciousness of Christ, the Teacher of the World, who watches over the evolution of all humanity.

The flames of the twelve inner groups are ignited in what could figuratively be called the body of the Teacher of the World. They are vivified and nurtured by the action of this energy and at the same time, through their own radiance, they attest to the potency of that body.

We are living in special circumstances, a time of great opportunities. In the present planetary transition, as well as in the evolutionary stage that ended on 8/8/88 (August 8, 1988), Christ, the Teacher of the World, stimulates and prepares human beings to become part of the inner groups and serves as the Hierophant[11] in the first two Initiations. From the Third to the Fifth levels of Initiation the planetary Logos carries out this task through sublime consciousnesses present today in the environs of the Earth. Upon becoming a part of the Inner Schools, a being is fully accepted into solar life and, working through certain intermediaries, the Logos of that system guides the Sixth Initiation.

The future Earth will come into manifestation under the light of the inner groups and of the Inner Schools. Each human will have established affiliation with his or her corresponding inner group. Broader contacts will open up to humanity. The sequence of the Initiations will undergo adjustments so that a new order may be fully established.

The Earth is reaching its Fourth Initiation. On a planetary sphere this is characterized by renunciation and by crucifixion.

---

[11] **Hierophant.** An elevated consciousness that acts as Initiator in the process of Initiation that takes place by 'external' stimulation, such as occurs on the Earth. It is responsible for guiding the energy that flows at the moment of Initiation so as to activate specific energy centers in the one receiving Initiation.

Therefore, the symbol of the cross is so timely, regardless of religious connotations stemming from erroneous interpretations. When human consciousness tears away the veils of illusion that separate it from the real, it will glimpse eternity. In this way, the horizontal beam of the fixed cross is revealed as the immutability of eternal life. The extent to which this is understood depends on the level where one's consciousness is focused.

The awakening of the monadic level is becoming accessible to a larger number of beings. The cardinal cross is being replaced by a symbol that carries the energy of the divine level, where the Regent-Avatar has its existence. This energy from the divine level is a key that opens the doors to the nonmaterial world. The symbol of the cardinal cross that reflects this energy is attuned with a more inward and esoteric aspect of Miz Tli Tlan.

Like a mantle ready to enfold life that is beginning, the substance of the different levels of consciousness, now under a new configuration,[12] will have the flexibility required by the continuous flow of subtle energies. The interaction of the Earth with the universe of which it is part, will be much broader and more consolidated. The intraterrestrial and extra-planetary energies present in each inner group will be more easily recognized.

The present era of transition heralds the new time. In the coming cycle, the crosses that until now have symbolized the different nuclei of planetary consciousness, will be revealed in different raiment because the energy shift requires the forms that represent these nuclei to be updated. In the silence of beingness, those who seek the truth must be open to these new times. If the task calls for it, they will find the symbolic images that correspond to these new times within their own being.

---

[12] **New configuration.** The levels of consciousness in which planetary life is expressed are undergoing a reorganization that is reflected directly in the constitution of the mental, emotional and physical-etheric bodies of human beings.

Human consciousness has evolved over the past few centuries. The advancement of humanity shows that it is assimilating inner impulses. These impulses determine the emergence of new symbols capable of expressing the level of consciousness attained by beings who are receptive to the light. Because of the heterogeneity still present on Earth new symbols will only be clearly perceived by humans in the future cycle. However, we can already begin to contact the beneficial radiations of these sublime energies.

✧ ✧ ✧

A Cristic Message

I was among you and you did not recognize me; I went to you but you paid little heed. However, I am now speaking to you again; I am within you; I come to accomplish what was promised to this humanity.

Even the farthest corner of the infinite cosmic universe is present in the Father's sublime consciousness; all of Creation is part of His Being. His Life sustains each and every particle that exists.

I did not leave this planet, nor did I leave you inwardly. You and I are one life, a single consciousness. The world of forms unfolds into multiple facets; essential life is integrated into the core of the Great Central Sun.

Receive my Presence just as one who is thirsty drinks of the water that is miraculously given in the midst of the desert. Let the yeast of gratitude leaven the dough that is ready to take on form within you and to be transformed into the Bread of Life in the heat of the fire of the spirit.

This will be the sustenance that you should give to the brothers and sisters who follow your footsteps along this path. You crossed a Portal; you fulfilled the necessary tests, now you should go on steadfastly. You will face new tests. They will make you grow; they are part of your learning.

I come to you to lead you to your true Home. Let ambition, the secret expectations of spiritual growth, wither away. I am your Teacher. I am the Teacher of humans and of angels.

I bless you on the path of the Initiations, a narrow path reserved for those who, in the purity of surrender, allow themselves to die to the world. These are born in Glory and they receive the garments that identify them in the Celestial Kingdom as Bearers of the Great Light.

You are the lamp. I am the light radiated by the Father's flame of Life, the flame that glows within you. The day is coming when I will not only be calling you to my heart, but we will have become unified into a single body. Great is the glory of the coming times. Hold these words in silence. You are on the way to the Encounter.

About Trigueirinho and His Work

Jose Trigueirinho Netto (1931-2018) was born in Sao Paulo, Brazil. He lived in Europe for a number of years, where he maintained contact with individuals who were advanced on the spiritual path, including Paul Brunton.

In his own life he was an example of the teachings that he transmitted through his books and talks about the transcendence and elevation of the human being, the contact with the soul and with even more profound nuclei of the being, impersonal service, and the link with the Spiritual Hierarchies.

One of the fundamental elements of his work is to stimulate the expansion of human consciousness and to liberate it from the bonds that keep it imprisoned to material aspects of existence, both external and internal.

He was the Founder of the Community of Light Figueira (http://www.comunidadefigueira.org.br) and a Founder and member of the Board of Directors of the Fraternity International

Humanitarian Federation (www.fraterinternacional) as well as a Co-Founder of the Grace Mercy Order, an ecumenical Christian monastic order. He also was an active collaborator, instructor and spiritual protector of three other communities located in Uruguay, Argentina and Portugal.

In his last 30 years he lived in the Community of Light Figueira, in the interior of Minas Gerais, Brazil, a community that at present has approximately 300 residents and which is visited annually by thousands of collaborators who are members of a larger network of humanitarian services and of spiritual studies that was always guided and followed closely by Trigueirinho.

Thanks to his inestimable instruction and his love for the Kingdoms of Nature and as a result of the exemplary work that he himself implanted in the Figueira community, the Animal, Vegetable and Mineral Kingdoms are the recipients of loving treatment there.

Trigueirinho wrote over 80 books, published originally in Portuguese, with many of them translated into Spanish, English, French and German. He gave more than 3,000 talks that were recorded live and which are available in CD, with some available in DVD and pen drive.

The primary focus of the first phase of Trigueirinho's work was concerned with self-knowledge, prayer, instruction and spiritual transformation. Following this, he began to transmit information with respect to Universal Life and about the assistance that humanity has from its beginnings received by means of the Intra-terrestrial White Brotherhood which inhabits the Retreats and the Planetary Centers as well as through the Cosmic Brotherhood of the Universe. He provides information about the presence of the Spiritual Hierarchy on the planet and the advent of the new humanity.

His work also includes themes relating to: the need for humanity to balance the negative karmas that it has created in relation to the Kingdoms of Nature; the negative karmic burden that we carry from the history of slavery and the genocide of indigenous peoples; and the nature of spiritual work in groups. He also addresses issues of healing, a larger vision of astrology, the esoteric nature of symbols, sound and colors, and the divine feminine.

In his last eight years he analyzed with clarity and with the wisdom that always characterized him, the messages that the Divinity has been giving to the planet as a warning to humanity (available from www.mensajerosdivinos.org/en).

His work reveals a real comprehension of the significance of all the Kingdoms of Nature on our planet, the true spiritual task of the human being, its place in the universe and also its responsibility before Creation.

Finally, he clarifies the reasons for the crisis that today is devastating humanity, teaching how to avoid reacting negatively to an immanent natural catastrophe by contacting more subtle levels of consciousness, and opening perspectives for the beginning of a more luminous cycle for our race.

Books by Trigueirinho

(Books available in English have English title first)

Published by Editora Pensamento
Sao Paulo, Brazil

1987

NOSSA VIDA NOS SONHOS
OUR LIFE IN DREAMS

A ENERGIA DOS RAIOS EM NOSSA VIDA
THE ENERGY OF THE RAYS IN OUR LIVES

1988

DO IRREAL AO REAL
FROM THE UNREAL TO THE REAL

HORA DE CRESCER INTERIORMENTE
O Mito de Hércules Hoje
TIME FOR INNER GROWTH — *The Myth of Hercules Today*

A MORTE SEM MEDO E SEM CULPA
DEATH WITHOUT FEAR AND WITHOUT GUILT

CAMINHOS PARA A CURA INTERIOR
PATHS TO INNER HEALING

1989

ERKS – *Mundo Interno*
ERKS – *The Inner World*

Miz Tli Tlan – *Um Mundo que Desperta*
MIZ TLI TLAN – *A World that Awakens*

Aurora – **Essência Cósmica Curadora**
AURORA – *Cosmic Essence of Healing*

Signs of Contact
SINAIS DE CONTATO

O Novo Começo do Mundo
THE NEW BEGINNING OF THE WORLD

A Quinta Raça
THE FIFTH RACE

Padrões de conduta para a nova Humanidade
PATTERNS OF CONDUCT FOR THE NEW HUMANITY

Novos Sinais de Contato
NEW SIGNS OF CONTACT

Os Jardineiros do Espaço
THE SPACE GARDENERS

1990

A Busca da Síntese
THE SEARCH FOR SYNTHESIS

Noah's Vessel
A NAVE DE NOÉ

Tempo de Retiro e Tempo de Vigília
A TIME OF RETREAT AND A TIME OF VIGIL

1991

Portas do Cosmos
GATEWAYS OF THE COSMOS

Encontro Interno – *A Consciência-Nave*
INNER ENCOUNTER – *The Consciousness Space Vessel*

A Hora do Resgate
THE TIME OF RESCUE

O Livro Dos Sinais
THE BOOK OF SIGNS

Mirna Jad – *Santuário Interior*
MIRNA JAD – *Inner Sanctuary*

As Chaves de Ouro
THE GOLDEN KEYS

1992

Das Lutas à Paz
FROM STRUGGLE TO PEACE

A Morada Dos Elisíos THE ELYSIAN DWELLING PLACE

Hora de Curar – *A Existência Oculta*
TIME FOR HEALING – *The Occult Existence*

O Ressurgimento de Fátima Lis
THE RESURGENCE OF FATIMA LIS

História Escrita nos Espelhos
Princípios de Comunicação Cósmic
HISTORY WRITTEN IN THE MIRRORS -
Principles of Cosmic Communication

Passos Atuais
STEPS FOR NOW

Viagem por Mundos Sutis
TRAVEL THROUGH SUBTLE WORLDS

Segredos Desvelados – *Iberah e Anu Tea*
UNVEILED SECRETS – *Iberah and Anu Tea*

A Criação – *Nos Caminhos da Energia*
CREATION – *On the Paths of Energy*

The Mystery of the Cross In the Present Planetary Transition
O MISTÉRIO DA CRUZ NA ATUAL TRANSIÇÃO PLANETÁRIA

O Nascimento da Humanidade Futura
THE BIRTH OF THE FUTURE HUMANITY

1993

Aos Que Despertam
TO THOSE WHO AWAKEN

Paz Interna em Tempos Críticos
INNER PEACE IN CRITICAL TIMES

A Formação de Curadores
THE FORMATION OF HEALERS

Profecias aos Que Não Temem Dizer Sim
PROPHECIES FOR THOSE WHO ARE NOT AFRAID TO SAY YES

The Voice of Amhaj
A VOZ DE AMHAJ

O Visitante – O Caminho Para Anu Tea
THE VISITOR –*The Way to Anu Tea*

A Cura da Humanidade
THE HEALING OF HUMANITY

Os Números e a Vidas – *Uma Nova Compreensão da Simbologia Oculta nos Números*
NUMBERS AND LIFE – *A New Understanding of Occult Symbolism in Numbers*

Niskalkat – *Uma Mensagem para os Tempos de Emergência*
NISKALKAT – *A Message for Times of Emergency*

Encontros Com a Paz
ENCOUNTERS WITH PEACE

Novos Oráculos
NEW ORACLES

Um Novo Impulso Astrológico
A NEW ASTROLOGICAL IMPULSE

1994

Bases do Mundo Ardente – *Indicações para Contato com os Mundos suprafíscicos*
BASES OF THE FIERY WORLD – *Indications for Contacts with Supraphysical Worlds*

Contatos com um Monastério Interaterreno
CONTACTS WITH AN INTRATERRESTRIAL MONASTERY

OS OCEANOS TÊM OUVIDOS
OCEANS HAVE EARS

A TRAJETÓRIA DO FOGO
THE PATH OF FIRE

GLOSSÁRIO ESOTÉRICO
ESOTERIC LEXICON

1995

THE LIGHT WITHIN YOU
A LUZ DENTRO DE TI

1996

DOORWAY TO A KINGDOM

PORTAL PARA UM REINO

BEYOND KARMA
ALÉM DO CARMA

1997

WE ARE NOT ALONE
NÃO ESTAMOS SÓS

WINDS OF THE SPIRIT
VENTOS DO ESPÍRITO

FINDING THE TEMPLE
O ENCONTRO DO TEMPLO

THERE IS PEACE
A PAZ EXISTE

1998

Path Without Shadows
Caminho Sem Sombras

Mensagens para Uma Vida de Harmonia
Messages for a Life of Harmony

1999

Toque Divino
The Divine Touch

Coleçào Pedaços de Céu
Bits from Heaven Collection

- **Aromas do Espaço**
  Aromas from Space
- **Nova Vida Bate à Porta**
  A New Life Awaits You
- **Mais Luz No Horizonte**
  More Light on the Horizon
- **O Campanário Cósmico**
  The Cosmic Campanile
- **Nada Nos Falta**
  We Lack Nothing
- **Sagrados Mistérios**
  Sacred Mysteries
- **Ilhas de Salvaçáo**
  Islands of Salvation

2002

Calling Humanity
Um Chamado Especial

2004

És Viajante Cósmico
YOU ARE A COSMIC WAYFARER

Impulsos
IMPULSES

2005

Pensamentos para Todo o Ano
THOUGHTS FOR THE WHOLE YEAR

2006

Trabalho Espiritual com a Mente
SPIRITUAL WORK WITH THE MIND

Published by Editora Irdin
Carmo da Cachoeira, Minas Gerais, Brazil

2009

Signs of Blavatsky – *An Unusual Encounter for the Present Time*
SINAIS DE BLAVATSKY – *Um Inusitado Encontro nos Dias de Hoje*

2012

Consciências e Hierarquias
CONSCIOUSNESSES AND HIERARCHIES

2015

Mensagens Reunidas
COLLECTED MESSAGES

Mensagens para Sua Tranformaçã
MESSAGES FOR YOUR TRANSFORMATION

2017

Páginas de Amor e Compreensão
PAGES OF LOVE AND COMPREHENSION

2018

Novos Tempos: Nova Postura
NEW TIMES: NEW ATTITUDE

2020

Versos Livres
OBRA PÓSTUMA

Trigueirinho's works are published by:

Associação Irdin Editora – www.irdin.org.br (selected titles of books in English, Spanish and Portuguese and CDs in several languages), Carmo da Cachoeira, MG, Brazil.

Editora Pensamento – www.pensamento-cultrix.com.br (titles in Portuguese), São Paulo, SP, Brazil

Editorial Kier – www.kier.com.ar (selected titles in Spanish), Buenos Aires, Argentina.

Lichtwelle-Verlag – www.lichtwelle-verlag.ch (selected titles in Spanish and German), Zurich, Switzerland.

Shasti Association – www.shasti.org (selected titles in English), Mount Shasta, CA, USA

Lectures of Trigueirinho with Simultaneous English Translation

During over thirty years as Founder of the Figueira Community of Light, Trigueirinho gave bi-weekly lectures (called 'parthilha's or 'sharings') that were recorded live. Audience members were invited to submit questions to him which were placed in a small box and brought to him by an attendant. Arriving early, Trigueirinho sat at the lectern, reading through and taking notes on the audience questions. Thus, his lectures often began with the phrase "someone has asked a question...." After addressing some of these questions, he continued with the theme chosen for the day.

Approximately 70 of these 'sharings' were later dubbed with English translations. His voice or the translators can be augmented or diminished by adjusting the right-left balance of the recording.

To access these audio recordings go to: www.shasti.org/instruction, then drop down the menu tab titled

"Trigueirinho Instruction" and then click on "MP3 audios."
A Book to Be Written
A New Viewpoint of the Monad
Alopathic and Homeopathic Medicine
An Esoteric Dimension of Power
An Overview of Current Life
Angels and Humanity – 1
Angels and Humanity – 2
Angels and Humanity – 3
Angels and Humanity – 4
Bases of the Fiery World
Beyond Fire by Friction
Beyond Imperfection
Causal Body
Colors in Healing and the Formation of Our Light Vessel
Deep Healing
From the Human Kingdom to the Spiritual Kingdom
Getting through Today's Critical Times
Harmonization and Androgyny
How One Begins to Perceive One's Inner Self
How to Understand the Planetary Disasters
Human Trials | The Trials of the Soul
Information on the New Earth and the New Humanity
Inner and Outer Figueira
Instruction: a Step beyond Teaching
Liberating and Healing through Colors
Life in Cosmic Signs
New Supraterrestrial Pathways – 1
New Supraterrestrial Pathways – 2

New Supraterrestrial Pathways – 3
New Supraterrestrial Pathways – 4
Niskalkat
Noah's Vessel
On Vitality
Our Response to the Cosmos – 1
Our Response to the Cosmos – 2
Our Response to the Cosmos – 3
Our Response to the Cosmos – 4
Our Response to the Cosmos – 5
Our Response to the Cosmos – 6
Preparation for the Path of Initiation
Reflections on Illusion and Rescue
Reflections on Inner Attunement
Seeds of Inner Transformation
Seeking to Understand the Self
Several Levels of Spiritual Reading
Special Paths and the Path of the Majority
Spiritual Entities and Hierarchies
Spiritual Trials
Strengthening the Bases for the New Cycles
Subtle Bodies and Templing
Supraterrestrial Pathways – 1
Supraterrestrial Pathways – 2
Supraterrestrial Pathways – 3
Supraterrestrial Pathways – 4
Syntheses, Struggles and New Instructions
Taking Charge of One's Process of Dying – 1
Taking Charge of One's Process of Dying – 2
Taking Charge of One's Process of Dying – 3

The Art of Living in Current Times
The Cosmic Signs Reveal the Teaching – 1
The Cosmic Signs Reveal the Teaching – 2
The Desert
The Earth – Degeneration and Deliverance
The Era of the Gigantic Wave
The Importance of Self-Control in Epidemics and Other Risk Situations
The Light That Permeates Matter
The Mystery of the Cross in the Present Planetary Transition
The Doorways of the Planet – 1
The Doorways of the Planet – 2
The Doorways of the Planet – 3
The Doorways of the Planet – 4
The Doorways of the Planet – 5
The Days of Tomorrow
The Heart, the Ego and the Personality
The New Life That is Emerging
The Plan of Evolution and Us
The Practical Mystic
The Seventh Ray and the Devas
The Spark from the Divine Level
The Transmutation of the Logos of the Earth
The Voice of Amhaj
To Be Universal – Part 1
To Be Universal – Part 2
To Medical Doctors and Therapists
To Those Who Pray – 1

To Those Who Pray – 2
Towards Self Consecration
We are Part of the Cosmos
Working Spiritually with One's Mind
Working with the Feminine Polarity
Working with the Rays

www.ingramcontent.com/pod-product-compliance
Lightning Source LLC
Chambersburg PA
CBHW022007120526
44592CB00034B/704